GUIDE TO RULE OF LAW COUNTRY ANALYSIS: THE RULE OF LAW STRATEGIC FRAMEWORK

A GUIDE FOR USAID DEMOCRACY AND GOVERNANCE OFFICERS

Updated January 2010

This publication was produced by USAID's Office of Democracy and Governance, Rule of Law Division, and published in August 2008. In this updated addition, DPK Consulting, a division of ARD, Inc. revised the document to include several case studies after field testing the Rule of Law Strategic Framework. USAID Task Order Number: DFD-I-05-04-00173

PREFACE

This document offers accumulated wisdom to USAID democracy and governance (DG) officers and other USAID staff who are developing strategies to address weak or inadequate justice systems. It provides a conceptual framework for analyzing challenges to the rule of law, as well as guidelines for conducting a justice sector assessment and for designing and prioritizing program interventions. USAID's Democracy and Governance Office (DCHA/DG) recommends that an assessment be carried out by any mission contemplating initiating or expanding a rule of law program. DCHA/DG can provide assistance in structuring a scope of work and carrying out the assessment. A justice sector assessment would deepen the analysis contained in an overall DG assessment and provide the basis for integrating rule of law programming into a mission's portfolio.

This guide is focused on promoting rule of law as a basis for democratic governance. It complements *Conducting a Democracy and Governance Assessment: A Framework for Strategy Development* (November 2000) by providing further elaboration on rule of law. It builds on an earlier USAID piece on rule of law, *Weighing in on the Scales of Justice* (February 1994), while focusing more closely on the links between the rule of law and democracy. Relevant background documents can be found on the USAID website at http://www.usaid.gov and the USAID development experience clearinghouse at http://dec.usaid.gov/.

Donor approaches to justice sector development have pursued a wide variety of goals. Rule of law can be a critical element of programming across all sectors of USAID programming. By focusing on it, USAID missions can ensure that legal frameworks are adequate and relevant laws and policies are implemented. A focus on rule of law also ensures that the justice system appropriately resolves disputes, protects citizens' rights and ensures access to government services. This guide recognizes the importance of promoting the rule of law to achieve a variety of development goals. More importantly, it is focused on how USAID rule of law programs can contribute to the broader goals of democratic and economic development, with particular attention to empowerment of the poor and vulnerable groups. We are confident that it will assist in developing clear objectives and measuring results, within the context of democracy and governance strategies. This Guide is further intended to encourage DG Officers to develop holistic approaches to promoting the rule of law. Focused, strategic and holistic rule of law programming will contribute to effective and accountable democratic governance.

ACKNOWLEDGMENTS

This Guide reflects the combined efforts of a number of individuals within USAID over several years. Gail Lecce, Michael Miklaucic, Thomas Geiger, Jose Garzon, Gerald Hyman, Cathy Niarchos, Patricia Alexander and Jenny Murphy, all of whom served in USAID's Office of Democracy and Governance, are particularly recognized for developing and refining the concepts, ideas and examples in this document. Other members of the Office of Democracy and Governance's Rule of Law Division, including Paul Scott, Kate Somvongsiri, Keith Crawford, Achieng Akumu, Angana Shah, Louis-Alexandre Berg and Richard Gold have contributed to this document. David Mednicoff and Rick Messick provided additional insight and comments, and Eve Epstein and Susan Pologruto edited the document published in August 2008. We sincerely appreciate DPK Consulting, a division of ARD, Inc. for revising the document to include the case studies after field testing the Guide.

Further comments and input from the reader are welcome to help refine this framework.

CONTENTS

EXECUTIVE SUMMARY

The purpose of the Guide to Rule of Law Country Analysis is to assist USAID Democracy and Governance (DG) officers in conducting a rule of law assessment and designing rule of law programs that have a direct impact on democratic development. There is a special focus on empowering poor and vulnerable groups and promoting economic development and security. Within USAID's DG assessment framework,[1] five elements comprise democracy: rule of law; consensus; competition; inclusion; and good governance. This Guide presents a strategic framework for conceptualizing the rule of law, analyzing a country's strengths and weaknesses with regard to rule of law, and designing strategic programs to address rule of law challenges. It will help DG officers maximize the impact of rule of law programs on democracy and governance strategic objectives.

The Guide reflects the understanding that the justice sector is part of the larger political context. Effective rule of law programming may need to look beyond traditional approaches that focus on operations of the courts and other components of the justice system. When the goal is democratic governance, the analysis that informs rule of law program decisions must be broad and comprehensive, and programming must reflect a holistic appreciation of country dynamics.

This Guide is organized into three parts:

- Part I provides a conceptual framework for analyzing the rule of law, by defining the rule of law and highlighting the links between rule of law and democracy. The conceptual framework focuses on five essential elements of the rule of law and the legal framework, institutions and actors that make up the justice system.

- Part II outlines a four-step process for conducting a rule of law assessment. This process enables DG officers to determine whether rule of law programs should take place outside as well as within justice sector institutions, depending on country conditions. By analyzing the sector with respect to the five essential elements, it helps to focus attention on the key rule of law challenges as a basis for designing strategic programs. The assessment process should be participatory with key stakeholders, so as to obtain buy-in from the beginning of the process and benefit from their knowledge of local conditions and problems facing the justice system. This will also help develop the political will for justice reform. Appendix A presents illustrative questions to guide the assessment process.

- Part III provides guidance for prioritizing among the five essential rule of law elements and suggests programming options to address weaknesses in each element.

Essential Elements of the Rule of Law

Five elements comprise the rule of law.[2] Each must be present for rule of law to prevail. The elements are:

- **Order and security**—Rule of law cannot flourish in crime-ridden environments or where public order breaks down and citizens fear for their safety. The executive branch has immediate responsibility for order and security, but the judiciary has an important role as well in protecting rights and providing for the peaceful resolution of disputes. In addition, informal methods of

---

[1] USAID, *Conducting a DG Assessment: A Framework for Strategy Development*, November 2000.
[2] There is no single definition of the "rule of law". However, this definition which has been adopted by USAID is consistent with internationally accepted principles.

resolving disputes, such as mediation or truth and reconciliation commissions, can promote order and security.

- **Legitimacy**—Laws are legitimate when they represent societal consensus. Legitimacy addresses both the substance of the law and the process by which it is developed. This process must be open and democratic. In some societies, legitimacy can be derived through religion, traditions, customs, or other means. Laws do not need to written in order to be legitimate, since traditional/customary laws are often passed on through oral traditions.

- **Checks and balances**—The rule of law depends on a separation of governmental powers among both branches and levels of government. An independent judiciary is seen as an important "check." At the same time, checks and balances make the judiciary accountable to other branches of government. Like all branches, the judiciary is also accountable to the public. An independent and strong bar association can also help support the judiciary and serve as a check against judicial power.

- **Fairness**—Fairness consists of four sub-elements: (1) equal application of the law, (2) procedural fairness, (3) protection of human rights and civil liberties, and (4) access to justice. These sub-elements are key to empowering the poor and disadvantaged, including women. The justice sector bears primary responsibility for ensuring that these sub-elements are in place and implemented.

- **Effective application**—This element pertains to enforcing and applying laws. Without consistent enforcement and application for all citizens and other inhabitants, there can be no rule of law. The judiciary is an important element of the enforcement process.

The essential elements of the rule of law and the justice sector are mutually reinforcing in consolidating democracy. In practice, some elements of the rule of law are always present, but in some societies the essential elements listed below are relatively stronger than in others.

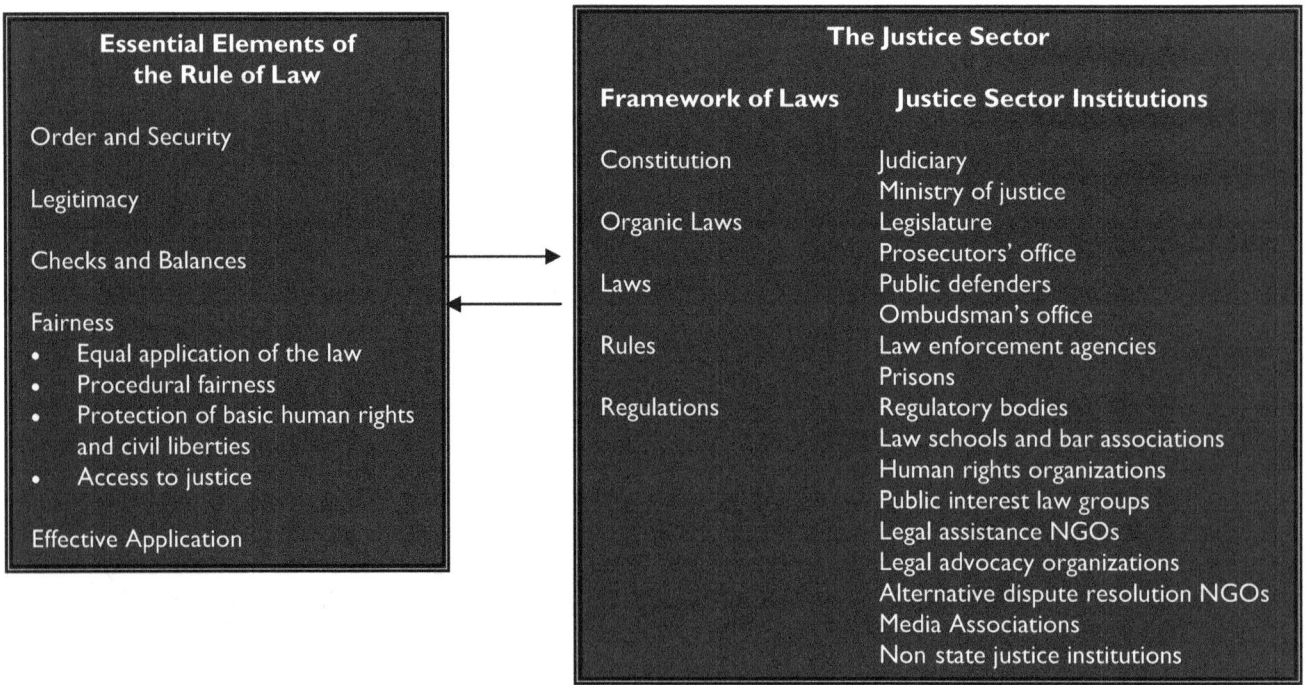

Conducting a Rule of Law Assessment

The objective of this assessment process is to focus first on identifying the key problems that undermine the rule of law and only then on the programming solutions, rather than using potential programming solutions as the starting point for program design. The four steps are:

Step 1. Take into account the political and historical context.—This step helps identify events that shape the environment, such as a recent conflict or the creation of a new state. It also develops information on the country's legal traditions and the origins of its current laws, both statutory and traditional/customary.

Step 2. Understand the roles of major players and political will.—This step helps identify the roles, resources, and interests of those who might potentially support reform as well as those who stand to benefit from retaining the *status quo*. It also guides an assessment of the strength of political will for reform and options for capitalizing on it, strengthening it, or working around its absence (or opposition). It is also important to consult with local implementing partners and other donors to understand the types of justice sector programs currently being funded or planned.

Step 3. Examine program options beyond the justice sector.—This step broadens the assessment beyond justice sector institutions to the overall polity. It helps determine the extent to which the effectiveness of rule of law programming might increase by supporting other initiatives, such as political party development or legislative strengthening, or educational, job, and health programs that are part of a larger crime prevention strategy.

Step 4. Assess the justice sector.—This step provides for a structured assessment of each essential element in terms of the two components of the justice sector, the legal framework and the justice institutions.

Developing a Strategy for Justice Sector programming

The assessment should identify the key challenges to be addressed through justice sector programming. Once the priority elements have been identified, programs should be targeted toward all of the appropriate laws, institutions, and actors that can contribute to addressing the weaknesses in that element.

Although country circumstances will vary, in considering the rule of law overall and its relationship to democracy, there may be priorities among the five essential elements. Two elements, order and security and legitimacy, often comprise the highest priority because they establish democratic legal authority. Two elements, checks and balances and fairness, may comprise the second highest priority because they guarantee rights and the democratic process. A third priority, effective application, improves the provision of justice services.

However, this priority sequencing does not apply in every context. For example, in sub-Saharan African countries, legitimacy may have limited importance because in areas outside of major cities, citizens, and sometimes police, do not have access to statutory legal codes. Arguably, law may not be legitimate if people cannot read or do not have access to legal codes, or police cannot travel to crime scenes for days or weeks after crimes are committed. Here, access may be just as important to legitimacy as it is to fairness.

These priorities should not be confused with mandatory sequencing. Other elements may deserve priority attention for a particular country, based on the specific rule of law challenges in that country, as determined through the assessment. Country conditions and funding limitations may not permit addressing the highest priorities first. When addressing a lower priority first, however, programming should set the stage for improvements in higher priority elements.

INTRODUCTION

There is growing recognition among donors that promoting democratic governance rooted in the rule of law contributes to long-term, sustainable economic and social development. Although the importance of the rule of law is highlighted throughout development literature, the objectives of various donors in supporting legal and justice sector programs vary a great deal. While recognizing the value of promoting the rule of law to achieve a variety of development goals, this Guide focuses specifically on the link between the rule of law and democratic governance, with particular attention to the empowerment of the poor. In doing so, it facilitates the design of rule of law strategies that contribute to democratic governance. Improving the rule of law can also have positive contributions in other areas such as security and economic development.

USAID's *Conducting a DG Assessment: A Framework for Strategy Development* (November 2000) identifies the rule of law as one of the five key elements of democracy. This Guide builds on that framework by providing a more specific conceptual framework for analyzing the rule of law, conducting a rule of law assessment and designing rule of law strategies. A revised version of USAID's "Conducting a DG Assessment" is currently under review and will be available in winter 2010.

> **Elements of Democratic Governance**
>
> - Rule of law
> - Competition
> - Consensus
> - Inclusion
> - Good governance

It also broadens analysis around rule of law programming. As the *DG Assessment Framework* points out, the reasons a country may have deficiencies in its rule of law are complex. In fact, problems that show up in the legal and judicial systems rarely start there. The justice sector reflects underlying power structures that affect broader governance dynamics. It also reflects the problems with consensus, competition, and inclusion that affect other aspects of democratic governance. Achieving the rule of law involves every branch of government at every level, business entities, political parties, civil society, and individual citizens.

This Guide looks at the full range of options for addressing rule of law problems and treats the justice system as part of the larger political scheme. Addressing deficiencies in the courts, laws, and formal justice sector institutions may be critical to promoting the rule of law. However, other complex problems, such as poverty, social exclusion, and government weakness, may fundamentally impinge on the rule of law. The framework reflected in this Guide encourages looking outside the justice sector to consider how programming in other sectors or areas of democracy and governance might support rule of law objectives. It also recommends involving actors across government and throughout society in efforts to improve the legal framework and justice sector institutions.

Finally, the Guide does not make any recommendations about how to sequence different programs, since country circumstances are too variable to make general prescriptions. However, it does suggest an approach to prioritizing rule of law programming, depending on the country context. It further suggests a range of potential programmatic approaches to address specific types of problems in the rule of law.

PART I.   CONCEPTUAL FRAMEWORK FOR THE RULE OF LAW

A. Definition of the Rule of Law

The term "rule of law" is used frequently in reference to a wide variety of desired end states. Neither scholars nor practitioners have settled upon an accepted definition. However, the term usually refers to a state in which citizens, corporations, and the state itself obey the law, and the laws are derived from a democratic consensus. This is captured in a definition proposed by the United Nations.[3] The report containing this definition then suggests certain characteristics of the rule of law, including adherence to the principles of supremacy of law, equality before the law, fairness in application, separation of powers, participation in decision-making, legal certainty, avoidance of arbitrariness, and procedural and legal transparency. The U.S. State Department's website similarly describes rule of law as protecting "fundamental political, social, and economic rights" and distinguishes between rule *of* law versus rule *by* law in more authoritarian societies.[4]

> **UN Definition of Rule of Law**
>
> "The rule of law ... refers to a principle of governance in which all persons, institutions and entities, public and private, including the State itself, are accountable to laws that are publicly promulgated, equally enforced and independently adjudicated, and which are consistent with international human rights norms and standards."

Both descriptions of the rule of law point to a universality of the principle. The rule of law is not Western, European or American. It is available to all societies. States differ in terms of laws and the treaties they have signed with respect to human rights. Legal cultures differ depending upon history, with many countries basing their legal system on the civil law tradition and others (including the U.S.) on the common law tradition, while many countries include elements of both traditions and may incorporate significant traditional, religious, or customary components. In many countries, religious law provides the foundation for family and other laws. Societies differ in terms of the values they ascribe to law versus other means of social organization, such as personal or family loyalty. Respect for specific laws and other norms varies depending upon cultures and circumstances. The principle of rule of law, however, transcends all these differences.

This has important implications for practitioners. If the rule of law is a universal principle, then supporting the rule of law is not necessarily imposing foreign ideas on a society. The challenge is to find ways in which a society may govern itself under the rule of law, using an approach that reflects the values and norms of that society. Indeed, countries which have successfully reformed their legal systems have owned their reforms by consciously borrowing from existing models, while introducing innovations where necessary.

---

[3] United Nations Security Council, *The Rule of Law and Transitional Justice in Conflict and Post Conflict Societies: Report of the Secretary General,* August 23, 2004, pg. 4, para 6.
[4] U.S. Department of State [http://usinfo.state.gov/products/pubs/principles/law.htm]

B. The Rule of Law and Democracy

Unlike authoritarian states, which may be governed either by law or by personal power or loyalty, democracies require the rule of law. The rule of law is important to democracy because it establishes the foundation for certain conditions on which democracy depends.

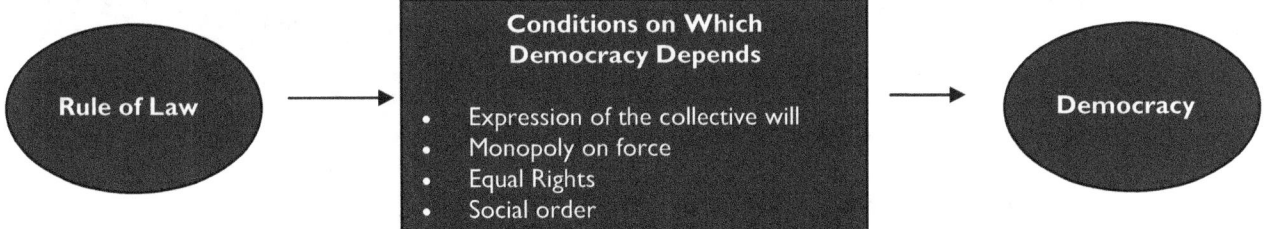

- **Expression of the collective will**—One characteristic of democracies is that law is a means by which the collective will of the people is expressed. An end result of the political process is laws that determine the allocation of public resources, empower public officials to act on behalf of society, and set norms of acceptable and prohibited behavior. If laws are ultimately meaningless due to inadequate adjudication, enforcement, or compliance, then the purpose of holding elections and forming representative bodies to enact those laws fails to be achieved. A legal framework rooted in the collective provides the essential foundation for these laws to be implemented and enforced. In many countries, the constitution is the highest level expression of this process. The constitution reflects the collective will of the people with respect to the organization and powers of their government and enshrines the basic human and civil rights that the people want protected.

- **Monopoly on the legitimate use of force**—Democracy depends on an effective state with a monopoly on the legitimate use of force. The constitution and statutes, including criminal laws, give the state the authority for a monopoly on the use of force, define when force is permissible, and restrict the use of force by citizens to limited circumstances. Without such restrictions, force and violence rather than consensus and competition may determine who holds political power, and those who pursue legitimate political activities may face intimidation or worse. Where journalists, politicians, and ordinary citizens fear to participate fully in the political dialogue, competition is limited and democracy is undermined.

- **Equal Rights**—Adherence to the rule of law levels the playing field in the political arena. Every citizen, regardless of his or her sex, race, class, or other characteristics, shares political rights and responsibilities that are recognized and protected equally under the law. Most constitutions ordain equality among citizens. Where the rule of law exists, all other considerations, such as class, gender, or ethnicity, are secondary. Where rule of law does not exist, other considerations may prevail, leading to a society with "second-class citizens" whose rights are not respected despite the formal norm of equality.

- **Social order**—The rule of law provides a stable basis for democracy to develop. It ensures the protection of those rights critical to maintaining an orderly and productive society, creating the conditions that enable a democratic society to develop and thrive. These rights are essential to maintaining basic social order and discouraging the resort to vigilantism, criminality, and violence. They include effective protection of fundamental property and contractual rights, guarantees of freedom of association and civil liberties, ensuring compensation for wrongs, enforcement and regulation of social responsibilities and obligations, protection of individuals against predatory business practices, protection from economic and social discrimination, and peaceful resolution of disputes. Such rights are also essential to ensuring economic development and addressing poverty.

C. The Essential Elements of the Rule of Law

Five elements comprise the rule of law. Each must be present for the rule of law to prevail.

(1) Order and Security

As the *DG Assessment Framework* points out, personal security is paramount to most people. In countries where public order breaks down or crime becomes epidemic, citizens may lose faith in their government. In the worst cases, they begin to take the law into their own hands. For example, lax law enforcement in urban slums and isolated rural areas has led to high rates of vigilantism in some Latin American countries. Similarly, climates of fear and frustration with high levels of crime can lead to calls for draconian measures, like the suspension of human rights, and to support for authoritarian leaders who can restore order. Failure of the courts to protect property rights adequately and consistently, to facilitate the conduct of essential economic activity, or to resolve disputes in a fair and timely manner can also lead to social unrest and black or gray market activity. It can also result in potentially violent self-help conduct, seriously undermining public order, safety, and security. While the judiciary and legislature have important roles in preserving order and security, the executive branch has the immediate responsibility in this area. An important and growing area for resolving disputes involve informal methods, such as mediation or arbitration, and other forums to provide closure after conflicts, such as truth and reconciliation committees.

Essential Elements of the Rule of Law

- Order and security
- Legitimacy
- Checks and balances
- Fairness
- Effective application

Case Study: Lack of Basic Order and Security in Nepal

The Nepal rule of law assessment concluded that the foremost challenge to the rule of law in Nepal, and therefore a priority area for USAID programming, is the widespread impunity that is impeding law enforcement, fueling a breakdown in law and order, and enabling crime and violence to proliferate. The assessment team found politics has been criminalized; crimes both small and large are regularly ignored; long-simmering disputes boil over into violence and retribution; and citizens regularly take the law into their own hands. Chaotic national politics have fed a climate of uncertainty as people wonder who is – and will remain – in charge. Successive governments exercise tight control of the police and government officials suspected of crimes put pressure on police and prosecutors. According to the National Human Rights Commission, not a single human rights abuse has been prosecuted in Nepal.

Where law enforcement authorities have the space to act, they suffer from limitations in capacity. Their numbers are insufficient, they are poorly equipped, and many officers lack basic skills. Low salaries, as low as $100 a month, create incentives for political pressure, corruption, and even involvement in organized crime. Investigative skills are limited and there are few specialized investigators. Prosecutors, who also suffer from insufficient personnel, limited training, and constantly changing leadership, rarely take an active role in directing investigations, resulting in relatively few criminal cases initiated in court.

The inability of the government to enforce, and refusal to respect, the law has fueled a growing lack of trust in the government and the legitimatization of violence as an accepted way to achieve political, economic, and social goals. Given the lack of basic order and security, the assessment recommendations logically focused on interventions to reduce political pressure on law and security institutions and increase their resources and training. These measures would be an initial step to support law enforcement authorities to replace fear with the public trust and confidence that are critical for democratic, public-service oriented law enforcement.

(2)   Legitimacy

The perception of law as legitimate and worthy of adherence underpins the rule of law. The rule of law as a basis for democratic governance includes not only the supremacy of the law, but a *democratic* basis for law that makes the law legitimate. That basis is that laws represent the collective will. In societies where the rule of law is observed, virtually all citizens obey laws, even when doing so contravenes their personal interests. This willingness is not based solely on the threat of sanctions; it also arises from the citizens' recognition that laws are arrived at in a manner set out in a constitutional order and subject to social input. Therefore, the laws represent the collective will. In that sense, they are "fair" and approximate the common good. Hence citizens generally respect the authority of law. Legitimacy can be achieved through other means; for example, in theocratic or customary societies legitimacy can come from religions or traditional practices.

Lack of legitimacy can occur for a variety of reasons. At the most fundamental level, when people have not reached a consensus on the basic boundaries or structure of the state, there is no legitimate constitutional order and the resulting laws have no legitimacy. Lack of legitimacy may also result when the process of proposing, reviewing, and enacting laws is deeply flawed. A legislature may be controlled by an elite faction, or its members may be so patently corrupt that there is no effective social input, and laws serve the interests of only a few rather than expressing the collective will. In addition, in emerging democracies, there are often questions about the legitimacy of laws imposed by colonial or foreign powers or inherited from non-democratic regimes.

> ### Case Study: Legitimacy of the Source of Law in Zambia and Morocco
>
> The African nations of Zambia and Morocco both have colonial legacies yet diverge with respect to the perceived legitimacy of their legal frameworks.
>
> The assessment team in Zambia found that the normative framework of governance in Zambia enjoys broad respect. The received law, based on English common law, and the customary law, based on pre-colonial traditions, are both seen as legitimate. The sentiment most often expressed in interviews was that the basic legal structure is generally adequate. The problems are seen in the refinement and implementation of the law.
>
> In Morocco on the other hand, legitimacy of the legal framework suffers due to the legislative process and the source of the law. Most laws are drafted by executive branch ministries and then forwarded to the legislative branch and laws tend to be amended or enacted with little to no consultation from the public. Laws are published in a subscription based Official Gazette that is not widely available. Another problematic aspect of the law-making process results from the legacy of the colonial body of laws that were inherited, together with the continuing practice of adopting foreign laws, sometimes with few modifications. This is particularly true with the commercial codes, where frequently the text of French laws is simply transferred into the Moroccan system – a practice that has caused difficulty, notably with respect to the law on bankruptcy.

(3)   Checks and Balances

Countries in which the rule of law exists have a
separation or diversity of governmental powers.
Excessive concentration in any one branch,
institution or level of government often leads to
the arbitrary and abusive exercise of power.
Separation (or at least independent decision-
making, if not complete autonomy) provides the
checks and balances needed to keep government
contained. Checks and balances occur vertically
among the different levels of government as well
as horizontally. When functioning appropriately,
regional and local governments can provide a
balance to central government authorities.
Through monitoring and oversight, civil society
also acts as a critical check on government at all
levels.

Checks and balances depend on all branches of
government functioning appropriately. In many countries in which USAID works, however, it is the
legislature and/or judiciary that needs support in order to curb the excessive power of the executive.

Checks and balances include the ability of the public to understand the proper functions of the different
justice sector actors, and to hold them accountable. This requires effective civic education initiatives and
a degree of transparency in both the decision-making and administration of public resources managed by
the justice sector. Judicial branch accountability also runs vertically, with higher levels of authority
holding subordinate levels accountable through the appeals and disciplinary processes. Independence and
autonomy of the judicial branch demand self-discipline to curb abuses and minimize the need for
external checks. An independent and strong bar association can serve as a check on excessive judicial
power. In emerging democracies, the judiciary often needs support in achieving self-discipline along with
the capacity for self-governance. Further discussion of judicial independence as a component of justice
sector reform can be found in USAID's *Guidance for Promoting Judicial Independence and Impartiality*
(2002).

(4)   Fairness

Fairness consists of four sub-elements.

- **Equal application of the law**—Democratic
  legitimacy derives from a consensus among citizens
  that laws, as administered, represent the collective
  will. That consensus fades unless laws are applied equally to all persons, regardless of their class, sex,
  ethnicity, or other characteristics. The most common failing in the criminal area is the impunity of
  well-connected individuals. The privileged may include politicians, elected officials, high ranking
  military personnel, members of the dominant social class, and wealthy elites. Unequal application may
  also occur when the poor and the disadvantaged, including women, are victims or the accused. The
  legal system often does not give such cases the same attention as those cases in which elites are the
  victims or the accused. In addition, unequal treatment can occur in civil matters, such as land titling,
  debt collection, taxation, landlord-tenant disputes, mortgage foreclosures, and enforcement of liens

and security interests. The poor and disadvantaged often have scant possibility of winning civil cases against the well-connected. In many societies, women are particularly vulnerable to unequal application of the law.

The reasons that laws are applied unequally are complex. Obvious flaws in the legal system (such as lack of judicial independence, severe administrative failings, or corruption) are only symptoms. The underlying malady is the power of entrenched political and economic elites who benefit from a compliant legal system or ethnic or regional domination. USAID's *Legal Empowerment of the Poor: From Concepts to Assessment* provides further guidance on empowering the poor through the legal system by enhancing their rights and enabling equal application.

- **Procedural fairness**—At its core, procedural fairness means that the government has established rules for legal proceedings, that those rules are fair, and that the government follows the rules in enforcing laws, thus impeding arbitrary action by the government. In the U.S., procedural fairness in legal proceedings is captured under the concept "due process." The Fifth Amendment to the U.S. Constitution provides that no person shall be "deprived of life, liberty or property without due process of law." The framers of the Constitution took this concept from the Magna Carta, which contained a similar guarantee. Although the term "due process" is a concept of the common law system, all legal regimes apply some version of procedural fairness. The procedures to be followed in both criminal and civil cases are set forth in criminal and civil procedure codes, which should conform to international standards for procedural fairness.

In the criminal area, procedural fairness generally guarantees the right of those accused of crimes to know the charges against them in a language they understand, the right to obtain or be provided counsel, the right to present evidence in their defense, the opportunity to hear or review the prosecution's evidence, the opportunity to confront and cross examine witnesses (where oral proceedings exist), and the right to a speedy trial[5], especially if incarcerated.

Procedural fairness in the trial of civil matters (such as land title, debt collection, breach of contract, and family law actions) ensures that all parties have a full and equal opportunity to be heard, to present evidence and arguments in support of their positions, to have notice of and an opportunity to respond to the case presented against them, and to receive adequate and timely notice of all court proceedings. Many countries have recognized a right to a trial within a reasonable time in civil matters.[6]

Procedural fairness is indispensable in controlling abuse by police and other law enforcement authorities. Where a justice system incorporates and effectively enforces adequate procedural protections, police do not easily or consistently violate citizen rights. The reverse is also true. For example, the failure of Haitian judges to enforce the constitutional requirement that an arrested person be brought before a judge within 48 hours to rule on the legality of the arrest results in the illegal detention of arrested persons by law enforcement authorities and violations of international human rights standards.

- **Protection of human rights and civil liberties**—Minimum standards for the treatment of all people and the preservation of their human rights and civil liberties have gained international

---

[5] See, e.g., Article 14 of the International Covenant on Civil and Political Rights.
[6] See Article 6 of the Convention for the Protection of Human Rights and Fundamental Freedoms (European Convention on Human Rights).

acceptance. These are defined in various UN conventions and declarations[7] as well as in regional agreements.[8] While equal application of the law ensures only that the laws, as enacted, are applied fairly, these standards apply to the substance of the laws themselves.

- Some governments maintain that international human rights standards do not conform to the values of their citizens. They contend that their legislation and institutions must be based on alternative standards of human rights and civil liberties. Determining whether a country meets the minimum standards involves a review of both the country's body of laws and the structure and performance of its legal institutions. The rule of law as defined above exists only if the national legal system both recognizes essential human rights and respects those rights in practice.

- **Access to justice**—Citizens have access to justice when they have the ability to prevent the abuse of their rights and obtain remedies when such rights are abused. Access to justice allows citizens to enforce their rights against infringement by the state or powerful private interests. Although a variety of laws and institutions are designed to protect the rights of citizens, if these institutional mechanisms fail, citizens must also be able to bring direct action to limit executive power and hold the government accountable. In many cases, the rights being violated are the rights to economic and social resources, such as land, title, permits, and licenses. These infringements often affect the poor and vulnerable segments of society, including women, who have the least knowledge of and access to legal recourse. The cost of initiating legal access, through judicial filing or attorney fees, can also negatively affect access to justice. Access to justice further protects citizens, particularly the poor and disadvantaged, against the actions of powerful private interests that may bypass or penetrate the state.

  For example, Nepal has a highly rural, broadly dispersed, and mainly poor population. Surveys have indicated that the majority of disputes that are adjudicated in Nepal are handled not by courts or government officials but by informal local actors such as village chiefs. Also, much remains to be done in Nepal to increase access to legal information such as statutes, government regulations, and the judgments and orders of courts. Very little of the body of Nepali public laws and regulations is published electronically and the Supreme Court has not yet initiated its planned Internet publication of its significant decisions. In Haiti, many citizens lack access to justice because they live in rural communities geographically distant from courts and other justice-related institutions.

  Access to justice is essential for citizens to support democracy. When the state fails to protect and provide for all citizens, and segments of society lack the ability to obtain justice, there will be less support for democracy.

---

[7] Relevant UN conventions and declarations include the Universal Declaration of Human Rights; the International Covenant on Civil and Political Rights; the International Covenant on Economic, Social and Cultural Rights; the Convention Against Torture and Other Cruel, Inhuman and Degrading Treatment or Punishment; International Convention on the Elimination of All Forms of Racial Discrimination (CERD), Convention on the Elimination of All Forms of Discrimination Against Women (CEDAW); the Convention on the Rights of the Child; and the Convention Relating to the Status of Refugees. Additional UN statements of principles and guidelines include: the Declaration of Basic Principles of Justice for Victims of Crime and Abuse of Power; Basic Principles for the Treatment of Prisoners; and the Body of Principles for the Protection of Persons under Any Form of Detention or Imprisonment.

[8] Important multi-lateral regional requirements and standards include: the European Convention for Protection of Human Rights and Fundamental Freedoms; the European Convention for the Prevention of Torture and Inhuman or Degrading Treatment or Punishment; the African [Banjul] Charter on Human and People's Rights; the American Declaration of the Rights and Duties of Man; the American Convention on Human Rights; the Inter-American Convention to Prevent and Punish Torture; and the Inter-American Convention on Forced Disappearance of Persons.

Increasing access to justice is not always about quantity—more court rooms, more staff, or more justice houses that must be sustained over time. It is also about quality—well-prepared defense attorneys, changes in the legal framework to protect women, better information, a computer terminal at the courthouse entrance that allows litigants or family members to see what is happening to their case, a more diverse and client-oriented court staff, and more convenient hours of operation. In many cases, it may be more appropriate to promote circuit-riding models where prosecutors, judges, and defense counsel travel to remote areas rather than spending millions of dollars to construct courthouses that people cannot reach. In Haiti, USAID has funded a "roving justice of the peace project" whereby judges travel by motorcycle to rural communities to adjudicate disputes or perform civic legal education activities. In El Salvador, USAID has funded mobile mediation units.

Case Study: Fairness in Zambia

The Zambia rule of law assessment team found that fairness is a mixed picture in Zambia. On the one hand, there is broad respect for law and the courts command a higher degree of public confidence than most other public institutions. The consensus of objective observers seems to be that "the country's judges and lawyers generally strive to remain independent." On the other hand, weaknesses in the performance of the justice system, combined with the widespread poverty in Zambia and limited resources available for investment in improving access to justice, raise serious issues about the system's fairness.

The poor (the majority of the population) cannot afford lawyers or the time and expense of protracted litigation in the backlogged formal courts. Public defenders and *pro bono* lawyers are scarce. For those in rural areas, the magistrate's courts are often located at great distances from where the parties live. The language of the formal courts is English and interpreters are not always available. Access to legal services from the government or from civil society groups is quite limited. All this means that for most people the only recourse is to the local courts. The local courts do an impressive job in dispensing justice rapidly and at low cost, applying customary law. Nevertheless, the well-to-do enjoy the luxury of a choice of law and a choice of forum – formal courts applying written law with representation by counsel, or local courts applying customary law without legal representation. The poor do not have that choice as a practical matter.

Unfairness is also evident in the criminal justice system. The poor are often held in pretrial detention for months and even years, while those with the means or with ties to the community, such as family members willing to post bond, are set free on bail. Despite recent public attention to the importance of gender equality to economic and social progress and the need to respect women's rights as a fundamental tenet of a democratic society, historical gender-based discrimination persists in many

---

Access to justice need not overburden state resources, because it is a right held in reserve. Most citizens—including those from countries with robust justice institutions—rarely step into a courtroom. Yet they enjoy access to justice in the same way as those with health insurance enjoy access to health care even if they never visit a hospital. If governance is sound and the rule of law is generally respected in society, then justice institutions can be used sparingly.

(5)   Effective application. There cannot be the rule of law without application and enforcement of laws. Even if laws are legitimately derived and equally applied, equality under the law will not occur unless the laws are consistently enforced and applied. Also, procedural fairness will not be possible since, by definition, it is about applying established legal rules to the government's proceedings.

The judiciary is just one element of enforcement. The police are the first line for enforcement of criminal laws. Fair and capable prosecutors must also be able to prosecute cases following arrest, which requires good coordination between police and prosecutors.

Executive branch agencies often have the lead role in applying and enforcing laws, through their regulatory and administrative functions. These laws and associated procedures apply to such functions as granting government pensions and other benefits, issuing business licenses, and enforcing health, safety, and environmental regulations. However, even with administrative agency cases, when these laws are violated or disputes need to be resolved, the courts and law enforcement come into play. In civil matters involving disputes between citizens that result in judicial decisions, either the judicial or the executive branch is responsible for enforcing judgments, depending on the structure of the country's legal system.

Compliance with laws rarely requires the judiciary's active involvement because relatively few cases

Case Study: Effectiveness of the Application of Laws in Zambia

The Zambia rule of law assessment team found that a primary rule of law shortcoming in Zambia is the ineffective application of laws. Some positive steps have been taken, including the creation of a "commercial list," an expedited and simplified system in the High Court for rapid adjudication, which has considerably reduced the backlog and improved the clearance rate. However, delays in the legislative and judicial processes and also in the dissemination of new laws and judicial decisions cause uncertainty about what is the law. Legal representation of the poor and the disadvantaged is clearly inadequate to the need. Judges lack legal or management training and often operate without trained staff, suitable facilities, or even basic office supplies. Financial shortfalls also affect the police, public prosecutors, legal aid providers, and prison services. Most prosecutions rely on police prosecutors who are not lawyers. The capacity of the police to investigate crimes, collect and present evidence, and contribute to order and security in communities is limited and popular distrust of the police is widespread. Forensic laboratory facilities and trained laboratory staff are lacking.

Both civil suits and criminal prosecutions incur unreasonable delays, due to numerous factors. Reasons for delay include rigid and unduly complex procedures, lax case management practices that tolerate excessive adjournments and continuances, lack of automated management information systems to facilitate performance management, the absence of recording equipment to create court records (leaving magistrates to prepare the record with handwritten notes), and judicial vacancies or absences in the subordinate courts.

actually proceed to court. However, the judiciary's role is much larger than the small number of cases would indicate. The fact that the judiciary and the other components of the system stand ready and able to enforce the laws serves as a deterrent and may be enough to promote compliance in a state governed by the rule of law.

(6)   Cross-Cutting Issues: Efficiency and Integrity. Efficiency and integrity are important issues that cut across all elements of the rule of law. Often uppermost in the minds of reformers, efficiency is a quality of institutional performance that can bolster performance in all elements. It is not a separate essential element but underpins all essential elements. Similarly, increasing integrity and overcoming corruption are extremely important to nearly all rule of law programs, but integrity is also a dimension of institutional performance, rather than a separate element. Efficiency and integrity may determine whether or not an essential element of the rule of law exists in a given country context.

In many USAID-assisted countries, such as in Haiti and Kosovo, the courts are severely backlogged. This affects access to justice and negatively affects the reasonableness of the length of the trial and the right to a speedy trial in criminal cases. The backlog of criminal cases may lead to a high percentage of detainees awaiting sentence and is often one of the most serious human rights problems. Backlogs of civil and commercial cases are also an impediment to economic trade, investment and growth and may undermine the legitimacy of the justice system as a whole. Typical responses to increase efficiency include introduction of plea bargaining, support to alternative dispute resolution, establishment of special commercial or criminal courts, automation, and improved court management.

While "justice delayed is justice denied," standards of efficiency are highly subjective and can be difficult to define through an international standard.[9] More important, inefficiency often masks more serious deficiencies in the five essential elements: lack of access to counsel, arcane procedures that create backlogs in one part of the system,[10] discrimination, executive interference or deliberate withholding of resources, or lack of security. What is important is that a rule of law assessment and design consider efficiency within *the entire framework* of the rule of law and from the roots of the system—the essential elements—rather than treating it as the core problem.

With respect to integrity, high degrees of corruption are symptomatic of inadequacies in the essential elements. These inadequacies account for much of the phenomenon of corruption. They include insufficient independence, accountability, and internal discipline (checks and balances); unequal application (fairness); or the presence of organized crime (order and security). Should rule of law programs target corruption? Absolutely. But an anti-corruption or integrity program should address the underlying problems that manifest themselves in corruption, such as bribery, lack of transparency, or lack of accountability.[11] Problems of integrity in the judiciary are not fundamentally different from problems of integrity in other branches of government. Pressure from civil society or increased community participation can motivate institutions to address these issues.

D. The Justice Sector

The tangible, concrete universe for rule of law assessment and program design is the *justice sector*. While the rule of law depends heavily upon the performance of the executive and legislative branches of government and on many non-governmental actors, it is the justice sector that is largely responsible for making the rule of law operative in society. Some USAID rule of law programs work outside of the justice sector, particularly when the fundamental problems cannot be fixed by working directly with this sector. Examples include a lack of basic order and security and/or legitimacy. In Kosovo, following the conflict in 1999, there was no effective judiciary with whom to cooperate. Thus, initial rule of law assistance involved helping to draft laws, provide infrastructure assistance, hire judges, prosecutors, and support staff, and re-establish a functioning judiciary. Most initial focus also involved executive and legislative matters, to provide the framework for a functioning judiciary and to establish order and security.

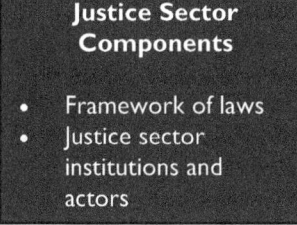

Justice Sector Components

- Framework of laws
- Justice sector institutions and actors

---

[9] Linn Hammergren, *Assessments, Monitoring, Evaluation and Research: Improving the Knowledge Base for Judicial Reform Programs, 2002.* See also William C. Prilliman, *The Judiciary and Democratic Decay in Latin America: Declining Confidence in the Rule of Law,* Praeger Publishers, 2000.

[10] For example, anti-crime laws that augment the power of police by removing procedural protections can increase the backlog of detainees awaiting sentence.

[11] See *USAID Anti-Corruption Strategy,* January 2005. See also Transparency International, *Combating Corruption in Judicial Systems: Advocacy Toolkit,* 2008.

The justice sector includes two interrelated components. The framework of laws is comprised of the laws and rules that govern public behavior, including the constitution, codes, laws, and regulations. Legal frameworks establish and empower justice sector institutions. They define institutional roles and regulate their behavior. Institutions and actors then give life to the law, which only exists on paper until institutions and actors put the law into practice.

(1)   The Framework of Laws

The initial evidence of a commitment to the rule of law is the reflection of the five elements of rule of law in a country's framework of laws. Legitimacy is reflected in the approach used to develop and add to the framework when this approach involves a consultative, participatory process. Since many countries inherit their framework of laws from a non-democratic past, legitimacy is often problematic.

A commitment to procedural fairness, access to justice, and checks and balances is most often incorporated in some manner in a constitution and then defined more specifically in subordinate legislation. This legislation contains provisions for implementing these guarantees. Examples include criminal and civil procedure codes as well as laws on the judiciary. Criminal codes establish the primary basis for the preservation of order and security. Laws establishing the authority for the judiciary, prosecutors' office, and police forces lay the basis for the enforcement of criminal laws, whereas the laws setting forth the authorities for executive branch offices lay much of the basis for application of administrative laws.

Most of the legal systems in Europe are based on the civil or Roman law tradition, as are the legal systems of many developing countries in which USAID works. The common law system is used in the U.S. and England and in some other countries following the Anglo-American tradition. In civil law systems, the civil code itself is the foundation of the legal order. This is because, in theory, enacted law is the pre-eminent source of law. Secondary sources of law, such as court decisions, are not binding in subsequent cases, either on the courts that issue them or on the lower courts.[12] In contrast, under the common law system, constitutions and laws are pre-eminent, but court decisions are also treated as important and binding sources of law. Over time, these two major legal systems are becoming more similar to each other by borrowing and combining elements and by adopting similar innovations. In addition, many systems include elements of both common and civil law. However, some important differences remain which can affect the successful transfer of practices from one system to the other. In addition, many legal systems incorporate elements of traditional, customary, or religious elements, either in parallel or as an integral component of the core legal system.

A good framework of laws will not ensure adequate rule of law in a country, but it does lay the groundwork. A statutory base that reflects consensus around the elements of the rule of law enables progress on all those elements. Additionally, in many cases, implementing regulations or rules are needed to define the specifics and mechanics for effective, practical implementation of the elements. In many developing countries, the absence of clear and complete rules and regulations is a very serious problem, often resulting in non-existent or poor implementation of the primary legislation.

Special Issues in Post-conflict Environments. Many post-conflict situations present unique issues with respect to the framework of laws. There may be lack of agreement about which framework applies. Also, the pre-existing framework may be incomplete or may not provide for fundamental rights. Post-

---

[12] Mary Ann Glendon et al., *Comparative Legal Traditions*, West Group, 1999, p. 125.

conflict interventions may include adopting previous codes or introducing internationally accepted codes as interim measures while longer-term reforms are developed.

The establishment of UN protectorates following the deployment of UN peacekeeping forces, as occurred in Kosovo and Timor-Leste, illustrates some of the challenges. The UN special representatives for these regions were officially responsible for adopting the laws that would apply to these territories. There are inevitable tensions in such an arrangement. For example, the UN Special Representative to Kosovo initially adopted the 1989 Federal Republic of Yugoslavia criminal procedure code as applicable law, a reasonable decision from the perspective of international law. However, that code had formed the basis for much of the discrimination against the Kosovars and was therefore repugnant to them. Consequently, the UN quickly undertook an effort to draft a new criminal procedure code and eventually enacted many new civil and criminal laws.

(2) Justice Sector Institutions and Actors

Justice sector institutions and actors, both public and private, governmental and non-governmental, make up the other component of the justice sector and the arena in which rule of law programs take place. Justice sector programs aim to reform and improve institutions. In some cases, this may involve strengthening institutions, while in others it may require moving in the opposite direction, to limit power. One example of the latter is limiting the power of the *procuracy* (institutions that combine police and prosecutor functions) in former Soviet countries by requiring warrants from a court for their actions.

The following describes considerations with respect to rule of law programming for key institutions and actors and also highlights special issues presented by post-conflict environments.

- **The Judiciary**[13]—If the judiciary is not operating effectively, it is highly unlikely that rule of law will prevail. The judiciary plays a key role in achieving all five essential elements of the rule of law. However, even if there are wholesale problems with the court system, it is highly unlikely that the judiciary is the only source of this dysfunction. Therefore, it is important not to program solely for the court system, isolated from other actors in the justice system. Capacity is

Public Institutions
• Judiciary
• Ministries of Justice
• Legislatures (especially the judicial committee)
• Prosecutors' offices
• Public defenders
• Ombudsman's offices
• Law enforcement agencies
• Prisons
• Regulatory bodies
• Public law schools and bar associations
• Non-State (customary or religious) institutions

Private Institutions
• Human rights organizations
• Public interest law groups
• Legal assistance NGOs
• Legal advocacy organizations
• Alternative dispute resolution NGOs
• Private law schools and bar associations
• Media associations

---

[13] As used here, the term "judiciary" refers to the courts, including judges, court administrative staff (such as court administrators and court clerks), and any associated staff under the courts' control (such as bailiffs and court guards). In some countries, prosecutors are included within the judiciary, and selection procedures for both judges and prosecutors are very similar. Civil law systems also use "investigating" judges, whose responsibility is to conduct pre-trial investigations of cases, while another judge actually conducts the trial. Investigating judges are typically part of the regular corps of judges, but are sometimes treated as a separate body. Courts coming from the civil law tradition may also include so-called "lay judges" or "lay jurors." These are citizens without legal training who serve on trial panels with regular judges, and function somewhat like jurors in the Anglo-American system.

often a secondary issue to political will. For this reason, training judges—often a favored first-line intervention—is not the answer to all rule of law deficits.

- **Prosecutors**—Throughout history, the role of the prosecutor has been very different in common law and civil law systems. The adversarial nature of the common law criminal system assigns a key role to the prosecutor. The burden is on the prosecutor to prove that the accused is guilty, and the prosecutor has much of the responsibility for moving a criminal case forward. In contrast, in the classic civil law "inquisitorial" system, the role of the prosecutor either does not exist or is an appendage of the judiciary. The judge is responsible for investigating the case, examining the evidence, and making the final decision.

  Many civil law countries have moved to a more adversarial system in recent years. In those countries, the prosecutor plays a role similar to that in the U.S. However, the legal systems of countries still vary greatly. Strategic rule of law programming involving prosecutors requires an understanding of these historical differences and trends.

- **Defenders**—Defenders, both public and private, play a critical role in ensuring application of the law, procedural fairness, and access to justice. Unfortunately for many citizens in countries where USAID works, legal defense is inaccessible because of either a lack of resources, a lack of a right to defense, or both. A critical issue with regard to defenders is the quality of their services and who oversees quality control in the defense bar. A strong and independent bar association can play an important role in supporting judicial independence and legal reforms, strengthening the quality of defenders, and providing a check on judicial power.

- **Police**—Police are an integral part of a system of the rule of law for the preservation of security and the enforcement of law. However, in many countries, police themselves have often threatened the rule of law by violating human rights, supporting non-democratic political structures, or engaging in corruption and illegal behavior. Donors are often reluctant to engage with the police, and historically police have received significantly less donor attention than the judiciary or prosecutors, with the exception of post-conflict situations.

  The growing realization of the importance of security to the protection of democracy in steady states, together with the continued number of post-conflict interventions, is leading to increased attention to police reform by the U.S. government and other donors. Until recently, legislative restrictions have largely limited USAID from providing assistance to police. "Community-based police assistance" was authorized in FY 2002, and legislation in 2005 considerably expanded the scope of permissible police assistance services "...to enhance the effectiveness and accountability of civilian police authority through training and technical assistance in human rights, the rule of law, strategic planning, and through assistance to foster civilian police roles that support democratic governance..."[14] Congress has renewed this authority in each subsequent Foreign Operations appropriations act. *Assistance for Civilian Policing, USAID Policy Guidance* (December 2005) provides policy guidelines and other information on police programming. USAID is developing technical guidance for engaging with the police to promote the rule of law.

Prisons—Effective and safe prisons are essential to promoting the rule of law. The escape or release of prisoners due to inadequate facilities undermines the effectiveness of the courts and police and erodes the legitimacy of justice institutions. At the same time, ineffective or outdated prison systems can lead to

---

[14] Section 564(a) of the Foreign Operations, Export Financing, and Related Program Appropriations Act (FOAA), 2005.

serious human rights abuses such as torture or prolonged detention. USAID was restricted from providing support for prisons due to Section 660 of the Foreign Assistance Act (FAA). Section 534(b)(3)(D) of the FAA, adopted in 1985, authorizes the use of ESF for "programs, conducted through multilateral or regional institutions, to improve penal institutions and the rehabilitation of offenders." This provision has been in the Act since 1985. Another exception to this prohibition was made in the FY 2008 Appropriations Act, allowing limited assistance to prisons and correctional institutions, including oversight and improving basic conditions.[15] This provision was revised in the 2010, State, Foreign Operation Appropriations Act (PL 111-117) to focus assistance to the governments specifically trying to improve prison conditions.[16]

- Legal approval must be obtained prior to initiating any activities in this area.

- **Non-Governmental Actors**—Supporting organizations, institutions, and actors outside the government is often essential to addressing all elements of the rule of law. Supporting legal professional associations like bar associations can strengthen the quality and effectiveness of individuals within the justice system. These and other non-governmental organizations can also provide citizen oversight over the justice system and serve as a powerful voice promoting the rule of law and maintaining reform momentum. Bar associations, law schools, and NGOs as well as the media, schools, business associations, and other actors may also play critical roles in advocating for legal reform and providing legal services to poor or vulnerable populations to broaden access to justice and deepen public awareness and respect for the rule of law. USAID recently funded a successful civic legal education program involving Palestinian children in cooperation with the Ministry of Education aimed at raising awareness of civic education and rule of law issues through a creative writing exercise on justice day. Rule of law programs should consider how all actors might directly contribute to rule of law reform.

- **Non-State Justice Institutions**—This term encompasses a wide array of traditional, customary, and religious non-state justice and informal mechanisms that provide dispute resolution and justice-related services, sometimes with ties to the state and governed by an established legal framework. Non-state justice systems are generally structured around community-based institutions which may provide easily accessible participatory, efficient, flexible, and culturally relevant justice. At the same time, these systems may be based on complex and informal procedures, lack transparency, and fail to uphold international human rights and equality standards, particularly with respect to women. Nonetheless, the prevalence of these institutions, their popular legitimacy, and their impact on the

---

[15] Section 634 (p) PRISON CONDITIONS: Funds appropriated by this Act....may be used to provide assistance to improve conditions in prison facilities administered by foreign governments, including among other things, activities to improve prison sanitation and ensure the availability of adequate food, drinking water and medical care for prisoners: Provided, That assistance made available under this subsection may be made available notwithstanding section 660 of the Foreign Assistance Act of 1961, and subject to the regular notification procedures of the Committees on Appropriations.

[16] UPDATED Provision on Prison Condition. Section 7085 requires the Secretary of State to submit a report on conditions in prisons and other detention facilities in countries receiving United States assistance where the Assistant Secretary of State for Democracy, Human Rights and Labor has determined that arbitrary detention and/or cruel, inhumane or degrading treatment, or inhumane conditions, is common, and identifying those countries whose governments are, and are not, making significant efforts to eliminate such conditions. The Act provides that funds shall be made available, notwithstanding section 660 of the FAA, for governments identified in the report that are making such significant efforts.

rule of law may make them worthwhile to engage. USAID is developing technical guidance on engaging with non-state justice institutions.[17]

Special Issues in Post-conflict Environments. Post-conflict conditions present special challenges with respect to rebuilding justice sector institutions. These institutions may simply be destroyed as a result of violence or civil war. Even if they are not, they may have little or no capacity to assume basic functions for maintaining order and security. In other cases, justice sector institutions have little credibility because they were under the control of disbanded authoritarian regimes and can no longer be relied upon. The post-conflict rebuilding process is challenging and complex. It requires strategies that promote local ownership and financial sustainability, and that develop local capacity quickly. USAID's Office of Democracy and Governance is developing guidance for several institution-building approaches in post-conflict environments that meet these criteria.

> **Rebuilding the Judiciary in Kosovo**
> In Kosovo, peacekeeping forces filled key law enforcement functions before the UN transitional authority brought in international police, judges, and lawyers to fill local needs. A judicial review committee was then established to vet local judges so that they could be trained and reintegrated into a local judiciary.

---

[17] A useful overview of programming options for non-state justice institutions is *Non-state Justice and Security Systems*, United Kingdom Department for International Development Briefing PD Info 018, May 2004.

PART II. CONDUCTING A RULE OF LAW ASSESSMENT

Rule of law activities often emerge from the urgency to address an obvious problem, such as corruption, crime, or a poor investment climate. Too often, activities are defined without the benefit of a systematic assessment that looks at all elements, their context, and program options. In the absence of such an assessment, sometimes programs become ends unto themselves, without ensuring their impact on broader goals of promoting the rule of law and democratic governance. In addition, the process should be participatory with key stakeholders. This not only allows the assessment team to benefit from local justice experts and ensure the accuracy of assessment findings, but also helps to create buy-in by key justice officials for justice reform. Positive change in the justice system will not succeed unless the local justice officials are truly committed to the reform process.

Rule of law assessments are intended to support the design of strategic and holistic rule of law programs. Starting from a broad look at the political and historical context as it affects the rule of law, the assessment moves into an analysis of the major players who affect the rule of law, before conducting an in-depth examination of the justice system itself through the lens of the five essential elements. This framework should help the assessment focus on first identifying key problems as they affect essential elements of the rule of law and only then developing programming solutions to address these key problems, rather than using potential programming solutions as the starting point for program design. In addition, the assessment should lead to a holistic look at the major rule of law challenges, including how factors within and outside the justice sector affect the essential elements of the rule of law, what options are available for addressing those challenges within and outside the sector, and what the realistic possibilities are, given the major players and political will.

> **Assessment Steps**
> 1. Take into account the political and historical context.
> 2. Understand the roles of major players and political will.
> 3. Examine program options beyond the justice sector.
> 4. Assess the justice sector.

The following steps outline a process for conducting such a systematic rule of law assessment. This outline is not intended as a practical methodology for conducting an assessment, but as a framework for analyzing the rule of law and developing strategies to address the key challenges. Information gathered in the assessment should be analyzed according to the steps laid out below. Practical strategies for gathering data may include reviewing laws, regulations, and other key documents, conducting qualitative interviews with key actors, reviewing statistical data from court operations and other institutions, and conducting or drawing from survey research about public perception and attitudes. Specific questions and methods should be determined based on the local context, objectives, and unique challenges of each assessment. Sample questions and a sample scope of work are included in the Appendix.

STEP 1. TAKE INTO ACCOUNT THE POLITICAL AND HISTORICAL CONTEXT

The political and historical context includes both past and current events. Often, recent changes frame the problem and prompt the establishment of a democracy-focused rule of law program. For example, in Eastern Europe and the countries of the former Soviet Union, the primary goal was to overcome the vestiges of the communist political system. In terms of the rule of law, the power of the executive needed to be checked. The judiciary and the legislature needed to establish their independence from executive control, in form and practice, and begin to contain executive domination, including the power of the prosecutors. In contrast, the inability of the judiciary or executive to check human rights abuses by the military in Latin America defined a compelling problem, within the longer-term historical context of authoritarian control. As wars ended and human rights abuses declined, high levels of crime and violence followed, requiring a broader approach to the rule of law. In addition, post-conflict contexts are unique and influence the range of rule of law options. In these contexts, security, provisional measures, and transitional justice to address past wrongdoings are high priorities.

Step 1 rarely requires starting from scratch. In most cases, the "state of the state" will be captured in a variety of assessments, including DG assessments. These should analyze the political situation, and help identify whether a regime is a democracy, an authoritarian regime, or a state transitioning from conflict. If it is a democracy, the assessment will note whether it is weak, consolidating, or regressing into authoritarianism. Where there is no DG assessment, country strategic plans, operational plans, country human rights reports, and Supporting Human Rights and Democracy reports provide an initial orientation. U.S. Embassy political officers can also help with relevant analysis.

One critical but often overlooked contextual factor is the tradition on which a country's legal system was founded. That tradition affects the basic structural arrangements and functions of the judiciary and related institutions. For example, judiciaries in some civil law systems are, or may recently have been, part of the executive branch and dependent upon the ministry of justice. The prosecutor may have a very dominant or very weak role compared with that of the judge.[18] Although structural arrangements have changed over the years in most civil law countries to enhance judicial independence, they often still differ in fundamental respects from those found in common law countries. In most cases, countries considering structural reforms will look to other countries with a similar legal tradition for models.

When reforms of laws are contemplated, it is important to know why the old provisions were adopted in the first place. What the original provisions reveal about the structure of a country and its values will influence the prospects for achieving reforms. As with structural reforms, changes in laws modeled on provisions from countries with a similar tradition are often more likely to succeed.

STEP 2. UNDERSTAND THE ROLES OF MAJOR PLAYERS AND POLITICAL WILL

This step develops information on the roles, resources, and interests of leaders and others whose support is necessary for rule of law reforms. Those working within justice sector institutions—the rank and file as well as the leadership—will always be important actors. They can either support a reform program or sabotage it. It is therefore critical to gain the support of at least some actors working in the system at all levels. In most cases, this is feasible. Concerns that inside actors have about reforms should be heard and addressed from the outset or they will likely turn into obstacles.

The most crucial and revealing question can be who benefits from weaknesses in the rule of law. Such beneficiaries typically are political, military, social and economic elites who protect their interests and status by undermining effective rule of law in the country. Understanding their interests can be essential to identifying opposition to reform and working to overcome resistance to change. There are usually some members of the establishment who understand that reform is in their long-term best interests. Such allies can be valuable counterweights to powerful stakeholders who seek to thwart progress.

The assessment should also focus on identifying non-governmental champions. Leadership within civil society and the media can be pivotal to success. Leaders of NGOs and the media can monitor government and the judiciary and push for follow-through on public commitments, thereby sustaining rule of law reforms over time.

---

[18] The Latin American civil law tradition features a strong investigative judge and a weak prosecutor; by contrast, under communist legal systems, the *procuracy* (institutions that combine police and prosecutor functions) completely dominated procedures. Reforms in both regions have sought to bring about greater balance in both roles while respecting other aspects of the civil law tradition.

The support for rule of law reforms is often characterized by the term "political will." Everyone agrees that political will is an important ingredient for the success of reform programs. However, applying the concept to program decisions requires some caution. USAID's earlier piece on rule of law programming, *Weighing in on the Scales of Justice* (February 1994), broke new ground in proposing a strategic approach to rule of law programming. Some interpreted it as making political will a precondition for working on the rule of law. This interpretation leads to a logical sequencing of assistance. The first step would be to build sufficient political will. Reformers would next launch programs in institutional strengthening, training, expanding access, and related areas.

However, political will is complex and nuanced. A superficial analysis, one based upon the actions or inactions of a few officials, for example, will not tell the whole story. The assessment must be sufficiently broad to develop a more accurate picture. Also, there is no fixed standard for how much political will is sufficient to launch a program. Moreover, governments and elites usually have a range of conflicting interests and views on rule of law reform. In many countries, elites and members of the judiciary and related institutions may have little concept of what rule of law reform entails. Their initial, uninformed expressions of support can quickly fade when they understand how reforms will affect their interests. Conversely, support may grow when the reforms become concrete enough to be meaningful.

While important to analyze, political will should not be a precondition for rule of law programming. In fact, rule of law programs themselves can cultivate political will. For example, in some Latin American countries, activities such as judicial training or providing modest amounts of supplies have generated political will and buy-in. Also, program activities themselves can educate and catalyze allies. Further, low-profile programs may gain a foothold before elite opposition groups whose interests are threatened can mobilize. In such cases, a public relations effort to boost political will could have the opposite effect by prompting powerful opponents to organize themselves.[19] Information developed during Step 2 will provide guidance on strategies to use political will, where it exists, or on whether and how to develop it.

STEP 3. EXAMINE PROGRAM OPTIONS BEYOND THE JUSTICE SECTOR

The rule of law is an end-state, not a set of activities. This step broadens the assessment beyond the justice sector to the overall state of the polity and its legitimacy. An understanding of this context will guide the DG officer in determining whether, for example, developing the judiciary is sufficient to advance the rule of law or whether it is also important to invest in improving political processes.

The rule of law is generally affected by the same underlying problems the *DG Assessment Framework* identifies as affecting democracy overall: lack of consensus about governance, lack of competition in political processes, inadequate inclusion of members of society, and an inability to govern effectively. Step 3 involves assessing how these issues affect rule of law and identifying some of the programmatic options available.

* **Lack of consensus**—If a legal system has totally broken down or there is no legitimacy, as manifested by civil disturbances or outright civil war, the situation may reflect a lack of consensus in society on governance in general. In these cases, programs that address the legal system will be a small part of broader solutions. One option is support for peace talks or international agreements to establish a basis for the rule of law. Another is to establish, train, and equip police forces and border patrols. However, only training and equipping police and border patrols will not establish rule of law. The institutional capacity of police must be improved and established within the criminal

---

[19] Linn Hammergren's paper *Political Will, Constituency Building, and Public Support in Rule of Law Programs* (August 1998) analyzes the fine points of political will, constituency building, and public support.

justice system so they can coordinate with other justice actors. Another option is disarmament, demobilization, and reintegration of combatants.

For example, the civil war in El Salvador was resolved through peace talks that addressed the broadest power-sharing issues, including rather specific details about the make-up of the judiciary and a new civilian police force. Reforms to the military, including the exile of a number of high-ranking officers, achieved with the help of outside diplomatic and military intervention, helped to build a platform for the peace talks and subsequent reform efforts.

In Afghanistan, the internationally-brokered Bonn accords of 2001 formed the basis for establishing a new government following the demise of the Taliban regime. The Bonn accords required overall reforms to the legal and judicial system; however, they did not fully resolve power-sharing issues with the warlords, nor did they resolve related issues such as the make-up of the new police force. Although a number of democracy programs are moving forward, the underlying basis for the rule of law was not yet established by 2008. This requires working at the highest levels. Program options in this case could include assistance in constitutional drafting, supporting the formation of a legitimate government (such as the *Loya Jirga* mechanism in Afghanistan), and contributing to broader diplomatic efforts to address security sector reform.

- **Lack of competition in the political process**—When there are fundamental problems with legitimacy rooted in the political process or the lack of such a process, prospects are poor for a rule of law program that works directly with the judiciary. Other options include rule of law programs that plant the seed for future reform, such as support to human rights groups and legal education.

- **Inadequate inclusion**—Elite capture of justice systems results in impunity and favorable treatment for elites (hence unequal application of the law, particularly for the poor and disadvantaged, including women) and stems from lack of competition and lack of inclusion. Therefore, any program that addresses these issues will also address the fundamental problems leading to a lack of the rule of law. Options include programs to support elections and political processes as well as decentralization and legislative strengthening. These programs help to build the checks and balances that characterize a democratic system governed by the rule of law. Anti-corruption programs are another option to confront elite capture of governance structures. Where the military is receiving favorable treatment, civil-military programs may help to support reforms needed to contain the military's influence and authority.

The neglect of the poor majority or minorities is another type of problem. These groups can be subject to human rights violations or lack access to justice because they lack the political power to demand their rights. Programs designed to increase their political power can contribute to the solution. Such programs may address political processes, legislative strengthening, civil society development, or decentralization. Other programs may focus on expanding economic, social, or political opportunities for poor or marginalized groups. USAID's *Legal Empowerment of the Poor: From Concepts to Assessment* (March 2007) provides guidance on promoting inclusion of the poor by enabling them to take an active part in political and legal processes.

- **Inability to govern effectively**—Where the problem is not a complete breakdown of the rule of law, it is often elite capture of the structures of governance, including those that implement the rule of law. In assessing rule of law problems, the tendency is to conclude that justice systems are "not working well." A judge participating in a USAID training program pointed out that this was an odd characterization, since his country's justice system worked exactly as it was intended to work. In other words, it was not designed to provide for fairness or transparency. This underlines the fact that flaws in the justice system are only symptoms. The underlying malady may be the power of entrenched political and economic elites who benefit from a compliant justice system.

STEP 4. ASSESS THE JUSTICE SECTOR

The purpose of this step is to rationalize decision-making about justice sector programs. Decisions should be guided by analyses of the extent to which essential rule of law elements exist as well as analyses of the extent to which missing elements are attributable to deficiencies in the legal framework and justice institutions. Assessing the framework and institutions in terms of the five elements will identify the key problems and challenges that need to be addressed in order to improve the rule of law. This analysis should also provide some sense of the relative priority of the problems confronting the program designer.

All too often, donors and implementers make *a priori* decisions about which areas of justice sector programming (criminal, commercial, or civil law) to address even before conducting an assessment. For example, if the local USAID mission perceives that the judiciary is an impediment to investment, then it will pursue commercial law reform. Program legacies, funding sources, host government views, and decisions within the donor community also heavily influence program choices.

However, justice sector programming options should be considered from the broadest perspective possible to identify the underlying dynamics and systematic problems that need to be addressed. These often cut across parts of the legal system. A comprehensive assessment will help identify a broader array of problems that impede democratization, thus informing justice sector programming decisions.

Therefore, the Step 4 assessment should focus on the five essential elements as they manifest themselves in legal frameworks and justice institutions, the two components of the justice sector. Appendix A contains a list of questions by element that will help determine the nature of the threat to democracy posed by deficiencies in the rule of law. These questions will yield clues for analysis, not definite conclusions. The answers will guide well informed judgments. Common sense is an important factor in the analysis process. For example, court management improvements cannot substitute for an independent judiciary; training in substantive matters cannot occur before acceptance of changes in law or practice; and strengthening prosecution and enforcement is inappropriate unless respect for human rights is also part of the reform agenda.

Good communication channels must remain open with other donors to determine their future programming plans and ways that USAID can complement their efforts. Host countries often request the same assistance from different donors, in order to hedge their bets.

Types of Data the Assessment Team Should Collect (See Also Appendix A: Illustrative Assessment Questions)

As in any research project, the assessment team should obtain data from primary and secondary sources that can be useful in analyzing the justice system.[20] The following types of data (if available) can be helpful in determining the efficiency and fairness of the justice system, legitimacy (perception), access to justice, resource issues, and help provide comparative analysis:

- A summary of the currently funded donor and USAID justice sector activities

---

[20] If possible, the assessment team may try to obtain some information in advance through cooperation with the local USAID mission. Pre-trip submission of questions or a pre-trip videoconference with justice sector officials may help the assessment team to prepare for the research trip.

- Caseload information (filings and dispositions/clearance rate for a specific time period and for discrete types of cases)
- Number of judges, prosecutors, attorneys, and police
- Number of complaints received and number of judges, prosecutors or attorneys disciplined for most recent year
- Number of cases investigated by police, number that went forward to prosecutors, and the number that were tried in court
- Presence of plea bargaining in the system
- Most important legal reforms on agenda of parliamentary body or ministry of justice
- Average pretrial detention periods for arrested persons awaiting trial, if available
- Conviction rate, if available
- Prison population, if available
- Number of specific types of cases (trafficking in persons, murder, war crimes, property, etc.)
- Comparative global data on key rule of law indices
- Number and condition of courts, prosecution offices, and police stations
- Extent of public information – trial schedules posted, sufficient notice, accessibility of court decisions
- Average salaries of judges, prosecutors, attorneys, and police
- Existence and functioning of judicial training academies and police academies
- Existence of integrated training that includes prosecutors and police
- Key NGOs involved in justice monitoring, advocacy, or civic legal education activities
- Information on access of minorities, women and disadvantaged groups to justice
- Representation of women, minorities, and disadvantaged groups in justice system, including high level positions
- Cost of operation of justice sector institutions and amounts allocated in national and local budgets both historically and prospectively
- Citizen surveys that show public's attitudes toward police, prosecutors, and judges
- The extent to which citizens use an informal justice sector (e.g., village councils, mediation, religious leaders)
- Sources of law in informal justice sector – e.g., religion, customs
- Extent to which informal justice sector conflicts with internationally accepted human rights standards
- Are sources of informal law written or oral?
- How does formal justice interact with informal justice sector?

PART III. DEVELOPING A STRATEGY FOR THE JUSTICE SECTOR

The justice sector includes the basic framework of laws as well as public and private institutions and actors that are directly involved in making the justice system work. USAID rule of law programming has largely concentrated on assistance designed to strengthen one or more components of the system.

Choosing the right type of program within the justice sector will depend in part on where there are openings for judicial reform. The justice sector may be amenable to reform when other branches of government are not. While justice sector actors (e.g., judges) are part of the elite in some sense, their interests may diverge from those of the executive branch, creating an opportunity to insert more balance in a political system. Further, it is not usually an either/or situation. Work in the justice sector can proceed in parallel with other programs.

Justice sector programs may also be an appropriate place to start for the same reason that has motivated direct justice sector programming in the past: problems with the rule of law tend to manifest themselves in stark terms in the justice sector. When a member of the elite gets away with murder, stealing millions from the public coffers, or violating the human or civil rights of the political opposition or minorities, it is clear that something is wrong. It may be much harder for citizens to focus on the underlying inequities in power and political structures. However, justice sector programs can generate attention to these issues, mobilize public support for reform, and begin to change values. Therefore, these programs should include a strong component of public debate and media attention. Working with civil society groups and community leaders can raise awareness of the role of the justice system in a democracy and stimulate the formation of a constituency for future reforms. It is unlikely that justice sector programs alone will solve problems stemming from underlying structural issues, but they can contribute substantially to improving the process.

Additionally, reforms in justice sector processes and institutions that build in transparency and checks can bring solutions, at least partial ones, even when underlying social and political issues remain unresolved. For example, when a court institutes a transparent case tracking system, it becomes very difficult to alter or steal case files, a relatively common method of changing the outcome of cases in many court systems. Another example is the transparency of the trial process under the new criminal procedure codes in Latin America. This has made it difficult for judges to find in favor of elite defendants when the evidence clearly points to their guilt. The public scrutiny it affords protects honest judges from threats and impedes dishonest judges from taking bribes. Also, depoliticizing selection procedures for judges bolsters their willingness and ability to decide cases impartially.

> Following the establishment of a new case tracking system in Guatemala City, the number of "lost" cases fell from 1,060 to 1 in the first year.

Another key issue in determining program options is resource and budget constraints. There will always be some useful activities—e.g., building courts—that will not be possible because the USAID budget for judicial reform for a particular country is not sufficient. Thus, key factors for the assessment team to consider when recommending program options are what is affordable and sustainable. In general, program focus should be on institution or capacity building, training, legislative strengthening, and improving efficiency in the justice system, rather than large "bricks and mortar" projects.

Section 1 defines priorities for justice sector programming in terms of the five essential elements. Section 2 illustrates the kinds of programs that can be undertaken in the justice sector.[21]

A. Priorities for Justice Sector Programming

When designing rule of law programs, a primary consideration should be to ensure all programs address the key challenges identified through the assessment. However, assessors must also consider the available resources and the affordability of activities, whether the proposed interventions or reforms are likely to succeed, whether political will exists for specific judicial reforms, and if there are local partners who can work with the rule of law implementer to ensure sustainability and local ownership. Emphasis must be placed on causation, such that if x funds are committed to y activity, then z (positive judicial result) will be achieved. Those activities which have a reasonable chance of success and address key rule of law problems identified by assessors should receive priority. There should be flexibility in the assessment approach, as the conditions and political, legal, and economic contexts vary among countries.

Country-specific challenges and funding limitations will define which essential elements deserve priority attention in strengthening the rule of law. In considering the rule of law overall and its relationship to democracy, however, there are often inherent priorities among the five essential elements. These are as follows:

First priority: Democratic Legal Authority	Order and Security	Legitimacy
Second priority: Guarantee Rights and the Democratic Process	Checks and Balances	Fairness
Third priority: Providing Justice as a Service	Effective Application	

Generally, the first priority elements establish democratic legal authority. If legal authority does not extend to the entire territory of the country or does not apply to all citizens or if the justice system lacks a legitimate foundation in the democratic process, then improvements to the system will by definition be limited in impact or will fail to support the overall goal of consolidating democracy. Order and security underlie citizen confidence in the state. Where significant parts of a country are under the control of armed militias, criminal gangs, or warlords, improvements to the justice system in the capital city may be helpful, but the overall goal of consolidating democracy will be thwarted by the corrosive effects on the political process of lack of order and security in the other parts of the country. This was the case in Colombia, where narcotics traffickers in the 1980s were said to have significantly influenced the political process. Where the laws of the land are inherited from a non-democratic regime, it does not make sense to train judges in how to adjudicate those laws; it would better serve the rule of law to focus on strengthening that society's ability to review and develop laws that are products of a

---

[21] Further discussion of programs USAID has financed in the rule of law can be found in the USAID publication, *Achievements in Building and Maintaining the Rule of Law: MSI's Studies in LAC, E&E, AFR, and ANE* (November 2002).

democratic process, and to train judges in the implications of the new laws. In societies where you have customary/traditional systems operating, the development community should seek to build bridges between the state/formal system and the customary/traditional systems.

Often, the second priority elements guarantee rights and the democratic process. These elements address the areas that are most central to the role of the justice system in defending democracy. For example, independence and impartiality of the judiciary are essential in ensuring the constitutionality of government action. They are also essential in such cases as election disputes and in libel and press cases involving government officials. Procedural fairness is also critical to democracy; politically motivated prosecutions are a favorite tactic that authoritarian regimes use to suppress competition. There are numerous examples of non-democratic forces using the justice system to try to gain advantage or destroy their opponents. The second priority elements deal with the processes that can protect against that.

The third priority element improves the provision of justice as a service. Justice is certainly a service. It has both effectiveness and efficiency components. The ability of a company to get a contract enforced or of an individual to get a divorce or to emigrate are all examples of the service provision function. This element is certainly critical to economic growth, but for a DG program one would not normally start with this aspect of the justice system if the higher-order elements were lacking. For example, one would not expect that speeding case processing in an authoritarian state would make that state more democratic. Indeed, it might have the opposite effect, making authoritarian elites better able to wield and consolidate power.

This scheme of priorities does not mandate sequencing of interventions. Other elements may deserve priority attention for a particular country, based on the specific rule of law challenges in that country, as determined through the assessment. A country may be sufficiently advanced on higher priority elements to enable focusing directly on the next set of priorities. In addition, for various reasons defined through the assessment process, it may not be possible to address the highest priority items first. A flexible approach is needed. For example, funding may be inadequate or too unpredictable, or strategic entry points may exist in addressing elements that are not the highest priority. Where it is not possible to address the highest priority for a particular country first, programming should be strategic, addressing a lower priority in order to set the stage for work on higher priority elements. For example, programs that deal with improving judicial system capacity to enforce and apply the law can lay the political groundwork for later interventions that address issues of legitimacy, checks and balances, and fairness. What is important is to keep the larger objectives in mind, capitalizing on windows of opportunity when they open to address higher priorities.

B. Program Approaches

A number of justice sector program approaches may support the strengthening of each element of the rule of law.

(1)   Order and Security

Justice sector programs can strengthen this element by supporting the following:

- **Establishing, re-building or expanding justice institutions**

In some country contexts, criminal justice institutions (courts, police, prosecutors, and prisons) may need to be established in order to provide the basis for an orderly society that preserves individual security. Examples of such contexts include post-conflict situations or newly independent entities. USAID's Office of Democracy and Governance is developing guidance focused on addressing rule of law in post-conflict environments. USAID rule of law programs can support initiatives related to courts, prosecutors, and police (within the parameters of *Assistance for Civilian Policing: USAID Policy Guidance* (December 2005)). Also, other justice institutions or mechanisms outside of the justice sector may need to be developed or strengthened to resolve disputes and maintain order. One example is a property claims system to prevent violent disputes over rights to land and homes that often follow a period of conflict and population displacement.

- **Crime prevention, community security, and civilian policing**

Establishing personal security goes beyond investigating crime and prosecuting suspects. The criminal justice system, specifically the police, also has a role to play in preventing crime. Community-oriented policing, with community involvement in problem solving, planning, and implementation, can significantly reduce crime and enhance security. Civilian policing programs reorient the police away from a focus on state security (protecting a regime) to personal security (protecting the average citizen). Community policing programs reduce crime by making citizens partners in law enforcement. Civilian policing and community policing programs focus on developing the services that police should provide to the public and on ensuring police accountability for those services.

Crime prevention programs can also focus on education. Examples include prevention education for youth, women, and families on the dangers of gangs, crime, domestic violence, and other problems. Another example is civic outreach and education to improve citizen understanding of the role of the police and the rule of law.

Community-driven strategies that address a broad range of local issues can help build confidence in authorities and help improve community-police relationships. For example, improving essential services, such as water, electricity, and education, as part of a comprehensive strategy, can contribute to crime prevention. The lack of such services fosters alienation and undermines confidence in authorities. Other programs provide constructive alternatives to criminal activities for youth and other at-risk groups. Programs that address these issues often fall outside the justice sector, but can be formulated to build confidence and improve security, thus contributing to rule of law objectives. This emphasizes the importance of pursuing a prevention, intervention, and enforcement model for addressing crime.

Police Reform in El Salvador

The rule of law program in El Salvador included a significant police component from the very beginning. The police lacked the technical, investigative skills to solve human rights violations that had attracted international attention, including two prominent cases involving American citizens. A special investigative unit was established and trained. The unit's ability to generate new kinds of evidence, including forensics, enabled police not only to solve more cases, but also to rely less heavily on confessions, thus reducing the human rights violations that had frequently accompanied them. Training laid the basis for democratic practices and the eventual establishment of a civilian police force as part of the peace accords.

- **Disarmament, demobilization and reintegration**

Programs that aim to take armed groups out of society by definition contribute to the establishment of order and security. These programs are often conducted outside of the justice sector. This illustrates how non-justice sector programming can be vital to establishing the rule of law.

- **Witness and court personnel protection programs**

In situations of high insecurity where judges and court personnel may fear reprisals, court personnel protection programs can be essential for justice sector personnel to carry out their functions and enable the criminal justice system to operate. Witness protection programs involving international relocation (especially in small countries where internal relocation is impractical) have proven crucial in prosecuting complex crimes such as organized crime, trafficking in persons, or gang-related issues. Although sophisticated witness relocation programs are costly and impractical in most criminal cases, alternatives rooted in community support structures or religious institutions can mitigate fear and intimidation. Also, most criminal procedure codes have less costly witness protection mechanisms, such as use of distance or anonymous testimony, or physical separation of the witness from the defendant. If the justice system cannot protect witnesses, they will not cooperate and fewer cases will result in successful prosecutions.

(2)   Legitimacy

Justice sector programs can strengthen this element by supporting the following:

> **Strengthening Non-State Justice Institutions**
>
> Research in Timor-Leste documented the operations of traditional authorities (*Lia Nain*) and analyzed them for concepts of traditional jurisprudence and dispute resolution. The assessment findings support initiatives to strengthen adherence within traditional systems to international human rights standards, gender equality, and guarantees in Timor-Leste's constitution and other laws.

- **Constitutional drafting processes**

Where constitutions and other fundamental laws were produced under non-democratic regimes, then by definition, legitimacy of the legal order requires that the newly-democratic society review the laws and make them reflect the current societal consensus. Programs can support constitutional conventions or referenda and can also provide technical assistance to the drafting process. The key to such programs is not a new constitution or law in and of itself, but rather the participatory process that leads to it. There is often a need for donors to provide information about international standards and comparative law. However, the consumers of donor assistance should not be a small group of experts without democratic accountability. Rather, elected representatives should always be involved, and mechanisms that allow for public participation and representation should be part of the program.

> **Reforming the Legal Framework in the Former Communist States**
>
> In the former Soviet bloc, the framework of laws not only reflected communist principles and practices, but it also incorporated outmoded elements of the civil code system that had long since been replaced by more modern principles and practices in progressive, democratic civil code countries. There had been no broad-based citizen input into the laws. In fact, for the new countries, laws were simply inherited, not produced by countries as sovereign states and democratic polities. The U.S. provided assistance in drafting frameworks of laws that replaced communism with updated democratic, free market structures. No country in the region had such a framework in place at the start of the transition. The new constitutions incorporated the principles of democracy, including separation of powers and protection of human rights. They also called for the creation of new institutions, such as constitutional courts and ombudsman's offices, to protect those rights. Perhaps most importantly, the process of drafting and adopting the laws was open to the public, carried out by democratically elected representatives and incorporated referenda so that citizens could agree to the new frameworks.

- **Legal reform commissions and citizen mobilization**

In designing programs to address the absence of the rule of law, it is important to include mechanisms such as legal reform commissions that generate society's buy-in both for the need for change and for the changes themselves. Complementary mechanisms include the mobilization of a broad-based bar association or NGO coalitions. It is often necessary to develop the capacity of these organizations to effectively represent their constituencies and advocate on their behalf. These approaches help ensure that the resulting new legal system reflects citizens' priorities. They also engender citizen support for reform.

- **Harmonization of non-state customary or religious law with state-based body of law**

Non-state customary or religious law systems derive legitimacy from tradition, custom, or religious sources rather than from a representative process. Their laws are generally interpreted not by publicly accountable officials, but by representatives of the clergy or traditional authority figures. Thus, customary or religious law systems, such as exist in Afghanistan or Pakistan, may not enjoy a democratic basis for law that reflects the collective will. Nevertheless, such systems do enjoy legitimacy in that they are followed and turned to by

> **Legitimacy through Citizen Engagement**
>
> In Timor-Leste, a National Dialogue on Justice organized by the Office of the President facilitated grassroots input on shaping the justice sector through district and national dialogues. Media coverage of the national proceedings reached citizens throughout the country. Justice sector officials are using the resulting recommendations in developing the justice sector.

majorities in many countries. The objective of programming in this area may be to bring aspects of non-state justice institutions under the realm of democratic accountability or to expand access to justice and human rights protections for vulnerable populations. This may involve elected representatives voting to include the systems in the body of state-based law. However, this may not be practical in some countries that have several different types of customary/traditional legal systems, such as those in sub-Saharan Africa. Alternatively, it could involve introducing international human rights standards into the non-state bodies of law. For example, revised systems might allow religious courts to have jurisdiction in certain cases, but prevent them from carrying out punishments that would be considered violations of human rights. Another programming approach is to provide for appeal rights from the non-state customary or religious system to the state justice system while keeping in mind any logistical obstacles. This approach can also protect rights that might not be adequately protected in the non-state sphere. USAID's Office of Democracy and Governance is developing further guidance on engaging with non-state justice systems and institutions.

- **Transitional justice mechanisms to address past abuses**

In post-conflict or post-authoritarian situations, a key to establishing the legitimacy of the legal order is to deal with past violators of human rights. The victims of such violators are unlikely to give their full support to the new political and legal authorities if those authorities allow perpetrators to remain free of any accountability for their past actions. While amnesties granted under peace agreements may resolve this issue, many contexts require programmatic mechanisms. These typically include truth and reconciliation commissions, tribunals (which may be international, local, or a hybrid combination of

> **Supporting Transitional Justice**
>
> Recognizing the importance of eliminating impunity, the Afghan Independent Human Rights Commission documented and collected evidence of human rights violations. A national consultation mechanism enabled citizens to provide input on transitional justice mechanisms.

the two), and community-based approaches, some of which capitalize on customary or traditional practices. USAID is developing guidance that details specific programming approaches that DG Officers can support, especially in post-conflict environments[22].

(3)   Checks and Balances

Justice sector programs can strengthen this element by supporting the following:

- ## Establishing or strengthening independent judicial bodies

Strengthening the power of the judicial branch vis-à-vis the other branches of government is essential to improving checks and balances. Establishing or strengthening independent judicial bodies, such as constitutional courts, supreme courts and judicial councils, is an effective strategy. For example, in the early 1990s, USAID helped several countries draft legislation establishing constitutional courts that have the power to review and rule on the constitutionality of legislation. Strengthening supreme courts that have a role in judicial review or administrative law also contributes to establishing a balance of power. Another focus is judicial councils, which are prevalent in civil law systems, especially those influenced by the French model. Judicial councils can have a range of functions, from appointing judges to managing judicial budgets. Their overall purpose is to make the judicial branch more independent and accountable.

- ## Upgrading or reforming judicial career processes

Many rule of law programs deal with some aspect of the judicial career, from appointment to retirement. They address issues such as merit-based selection criteria and promotion systems, assignment, oversight and disciplinary procedures, vetting, and the setting of salaries and benefits. The objective is to prevent the executive and legislative branches from influencing the rulings of the judiciary or limiting its ability to question actions or legislation of the other branches. Judges who are subject to pressure from political actors cannot play a strong role in guaranteeing human rights and democratic process. At the same time, these programs enhance the internal accountability of judicial personnel. The question of judicial independence and impartiality is discussed extensively in USAID's *Guidance for Promoting Judicial Independence and Impartiality* (2002).

- ## Improving working conditions for judicial personnel

These kinds of programs complement efforts devoted to the judicial career path. In order to raise judges' expectations of professionalism, raise the public's expectations of the judiciary, and attract qualified persons to the judiciary, working conditions for judicial personnel must be adequate. Without such expectations on everyone's part, judges are unlikely to see themselves as an independent voice and a check on unconstitutionality or illegality, and may be vulnerable to corruption. Programs that enhance working conditions can focus on facilities and equipment and sometimes on processes and procedures that define the working environment.

- ## Strengthening judicial administration, management and self-governance

In many civil law countries, the Ministry of Justice has traditionally managed the material resources of the judiciary. Many programs aim to remove this function from the executive and place it with the judicial branch itself. The objective is to make the judicial branch more independent and to distinguish

---

[22] "Rebuilding the Rule of Law in Post-conflict Environments" and "The Guidance for Democracy and Governance Programming in Post-Conflict Countries" will be available on the USAID Democracy & Governance website in early 2010.

judges from civil servants in the rest of the government. To assume these new authorities and responsibilities, however, judges need skills in governing themselves and their operations and in managing finances and other resources. Therefore, programs that develop these capacities strengthen the judiciary. Ultimately, the level of resources that flows to the judiciary has to be set by the legislature or executive, through the budgeting process or the Ministry of Finance. Some programs have aimed to legislate a fixed amount of funding that must flow to the judicial branch each year. This insulates the judiciary from political pressure exerted through the budget process.

- **Strengthening independent judicial and legal professional associations**

A judicial association strengthens the independence of the judiciary as a whole. It also promulgates the idea of the importance of an independent judiciary. Therefore, many programs either create or strengthen these associations. The ability of lawyers to practice freely is also an especially important principle in the context of many emerging democracies where former authoritarian regimes sought to control the activity of lawyers and curb their ability to use the legal system to check abuses by the state. Thus, the promotion of independent bar associations is often an objective of rule of law programs.

- **Enhancing judicial professional development and access to the laws**

Judges cannot uphold the law in the face of political pressure to rule in favor of the government if they do not know what is in the law or if their understanding of the law is poor. Yet, in many countries, judges do not have access to ongoing training opportunities, or to a codified, searchable databank containing all of the country's laws. They often have at best an outdated set of official gazettes from the legislative branch. Therefore, many rule of law programs support the publication and codification of laws and their dissemination through legal databases or hard copies. Other programs strengthen judicial education through establishing or improving training institutes and continuing education programs.

- **Stimulating citizen support for judicial independence**

Judicial independence cannot be secured by institutional mechanisms alone. Oversight and citizen awareness are also important. USAID has funded judicial watch programs, court-media programs, public awareness programs, constituency-building and advocacy initiatives, and judicial outreach and education to involve citizens in bolstering the independence of the judiciary. These activities have a synergistic effect. On the one hand, citizens watch the courts. On the other hand, the courts are proactive in familiarizing citizens with their work. Satisfied citizens then become advocates for the judicial branch.

> **Increasing Legal Awareness**
>
> Some local NGOs in Timor-Leste organize community-level discussions about new legal frameworks and laws. Others disseminate monthly bulletins to both citizens and government to raise awareness about new legal systems.

(4)   Fairness

Justice sector programs can strengthen this element by supporting the following:

- **Reforming and implementing procedural codes**

One of the most important ways in which USAID has addressed the element of fairness has been through criminal procedure code reform. These programs support the development of codes that reflect international best practices and human rights standards. While criminal justice reform is often important to fight crime, procedural reforms in Latin America have entailed wholesale restructuring of the justice system so as to improve substantially the chances of the ordinary citizen in the criminal justice system. Partly as a result of these reforms, several Latin American countries, such as the Dominican Republic, have significantly reduced their levels of pretrial detention. Lengthy pre-trial detention, sometimes exceeding the length of detention that would be imposed if a suspect were tried and found guilty, is a symptom of extreme procedural unfairness. Reducing pretrial detention does not necessarily require automated systems, but may be as simple as promoting better coordination between police, courts, and prisons.

> **Promoting Fairness: Criminal Procedure Reform in Latin America and the Former Soviet Bloc**
>
> In Latin America, donors have supported a movement to reform criminal procedure codes and the institutions that implement them. The reforms to these codes have addressed two fundamental problems: the power of the state vis-à-vis the individual, and the accountable use of that power. The reforms incorporated a two-fold approach: (1) to change the procedures for processing criminal cases from a written, inquisitorial system to an oral, adversarial system; and (2) to incorporate greater procedural protections for the accused. The primary purpose of introducing oral, adversarial trials was to bring transparency to the criminal justice process. These reforms had spread through several of the European civil code countries and were beginning to be debated in South America. Advocates argued that only when there were concentrated oral trials, where the prosecutor and defense could challenge one another and the testimony of witnesses and other evidence were subject to public scrutiny, would there be sufficient transparency to allow or force the judiciary to act as a check on economic and military elites.
>
> To enhance procedural fairness under the reformed codes, defendants were presumed innocent and had the right to counsel, the right to be informed of the charges against them, and the right to present a defense. Some of the new codes were also far more flexible in permitting release of defendants pending trial. This was a radical change for most Latin American countries and an extremely important provision, since up to 90% of prisoners in some countries were awaiting a verdict.
>
> In the former Soviet bloc, new criminal procedure codes provided a firmer foundation for protecting rights, to counteract many of the abuses that had taken place in the criminal justice system under the communist regimes. The codes incorporated increased procedural protections for citizens accused of crimes, including recognition that the prosecution must prove its case and that defendants can be acquitted. In Russia, to help counteract the power of the *procuracy* (institutions that combine police and prosecutor functions), USAID helped draft laws instituting jury trials. In

- **Reforming administrative law**

These reforms enable citizens and business to obtain fairer and more transparent treatment at the hands of government officials, thus addressing both procedural fairness and equal application of the law. Donors often neglect the administrative law area, but reform programs can do much to garner citizen confidence in government. Administrative law reforms can be specifically targeted toward addressing the needs of the poor and vulnerable groups by enabling them to access critical services, permits, and certifications. *Using Administrative Law Tools and Concepts to Strengthen USAID Programming: A Guide for USAID Democracy and Governance Officers* (2008) describes numerous approaches to administrative law reform. Some programs, such as in the Dominican Republic and Albania, aim to improve government transparency through helping to implement access to information "freedom of information" type laws and procurement processes, or to implement laws seeking to flag and eliminate conflicts of interest in the government. There is often a connection between administrative tribunals and judicial courts, since in many countries after exhausting administrative review a litigant can appeal an administrative-type dispute to a judicial court.

- **Improving transparent and efficient administration of justice system components**

These programs support improvements in case tracking and management (sometimes through automation) and in management and administrative procedures. They often address workload issues, slow processing, and backlogs. Although caseloads may not seem unmanageable by U.S. standards, many courts have experienced a radical change from the sleepy conditions they were used to a few decades ago. Additionally, as countries make the transition to democracy, the courts can no longer be rubber stamps, and resources need to be upgraded to meet new expectations. An important consideration in looking at caseloads is whether the procedural codes are the underlying cause for slow processing of cases.

Programs to improve transparent and efficient administration also support the introduction of public court hearings, the publication of court records, and the establishment of information centers. Most USAID programs address courts or prosecutors, and the new policy guidance allows for selected assistance to police as well. While these activities would seem to address effective application of the law, in fact they primarily address fairness, specifically, equal application of the law. A lack of transparency, inadequate record keeping, and poor procedures that permit a lack of accountability by staff allow for corruption and partiality in applying the law and adjudicating disputes. A classic example of addressing this situation is to introduce a system for automated, random assignment of cases to judges. This prevents parties to a case from paying bribes to have their case heard by a favorable judge. Discussion of program approaches in this area can be found in USAID's *Guidance for Promoting Judicial Independence and Impartiality* (2002) and *Case Tracking and Management Guide* (2001).

- **Expanding access to legal services**

These programs provide resources upon which citizens, particularly the poor, the disadvantaged, and the marginalized, including women, can draw to prevent the abuse of their rights and to obtain remedies when their rights are abused. Examples include support to public defenders' offices, legal aid, and legal services organizations and justice or legal resource NGOs. Programs in this area should be concerned not only with the quantity, but also quality, of legal services available.

Public defender programs play a critical role in ensuring equal application of the law, procedural fairness, and access to justice for indigent defendants, who comprise the vast majority of those accused of crimes in most developing countries. Absence of defense counsel is itself a violation of internationally accepted norms of procedural fairness and indeed of basic human rights, if the accused is charged with a serious offense.

USAID has supported public defender programs in several countries. Some have been quite successful, while others have had mixed results. The difficulty is almost invariably sustainability. In most countries adequate funds are not available or have not been allocated to support defense counsel for all (or for any) indigents. Moreover, because the quality of defenders' work is key, these personnel must receive adequate training, salaries, and incentives to curb high staff turnover that plagues most defenders' offices. This poses yet another financial challenge to sustainability. For this reason, public defender programs must focus on budget and resource management issues at the very outset.

It is also important to focus on the fact that the ultimate goal is to make the legal process and the court system function fairly. The acceptance of egregiously unfair treatment of the poor in the court system may in part be a function of funding constraints, but in many countries it also reflects attitudes about class differences. It therefore may be as important to include activities such as round tables, media programs, and law school discussions to examine the importance of fairness in the justice system as it is to provide universal coverage of public defenders.

- **Improving the quality of private defense**

Private lawyers are key actors in the legal system and are critical to advancing access to justice. As the American Bar Association/Rule of Law Initiative (ABA/ROLI) notes on its web page, "Maintaining a high level of professionalism among lawyers is a continuing challenge in emerging democracies. Substantive continuing legal education and training in trial skills are usually non-existent or substandard… Many developing countries lack a culture of engaging in proactive public advocacy." Program options include support for continuing education, objective bar examinations, and self-governance.

> ### The Role of the Private Bar
>
> Particularly in Eastern Europe and the former Soviet Union, USAID has helped establish continuing legal education programs to ensure that lawyers are prepared to offer competent legal services to their clients. Topics covered have included trial advocacy skills, law practice management, and ethics.
>
> Programs have also provided better preparation for lawyers just entering the profession. In Georgia, USAID-funded programs supported the drafting and administration of a national bar examination. In Kosovo, virtually no new Kosovar lawyers had been admitted to the bar during the decade of Serbian dominance. Further, many of the most prominent advocates for Kosovar rights had been killed or driven into exile. To replenish the profession and set the stage for modernization, law graduates were paired with practicing lawyers for a year-long internship to prepare them for admission to the bar.

- **Improving the accessibility of the state justice system**

Some programs support an increase in the number and geographic proximity of courts. However, making institutions more citizen-friendly, especially for the poor, minorities, or women, can make a considerable difference to access and may cost much less than investments in quantity. Measures to improve the quality of justice service may include: removing language and cultural barriers; changing court design to improve public attendance; creating a diverse and customer-friendly staff that communicates respectfully; creating one-stop windows and streamlined procedures; training mediators; publishing and disseminating laws and decisions; and placing information terminals or kiosks on the ground floor. Such relatively low-cost steps can make the difference between a citizen using the legal system to obtain justice or giving up.

- **Supporting or expanding alternative dispute resolution**

Alternative dispute resolution (ADR) is often promoted as a program to promote access to justice. If properly designed, it can "unclog" the courts and allow more people to resolve their disputes. It also provides an additional service that is easier to use and more appropriate and effective than traditional litigation for many types of disputes. ADR can be established within the state system (court-annexed) or beyond it in other venues, including building on established traditional mechanisms of dispute resolution. It costs less for the parties, who do not have to pay lawyers during a protracted judicial proceeding. A USAID-funded mediation program in El Salvador has seen impressive results. As of July 2009, more than 40,000 cases of the following types have been addressed through mediation services offered in public defender offices: family, business, community-based, labor, and minor criminal matters. 84% have reached a resolution.

Plea bargaining can also serve this role in the criminal justice system. A functioning public defender system can be key to assuring participation of the poor in ADR. USAID's *Alternative Dispute Resolution Practitioners' Guide* (1998) assists DG officers interested in developing programs in this area.

- **Increasing citizen awareness of human rights standards and issues**

In cases where the substance of a country's laws does not meet international standards of human rights, making citizens aware of discrepancies is a common approach to the problem. For example, in Kuwait, where women did not have the right to vote, the U.S. Department of State, through USAID, funded a program to train women's groups in public education and advocacy strategies. There are also many USAID programs that focus on family codes and their frequent discriminatory provisions. These programs increase citizen awareness of the existence of international standards and how the codes conflict with them.

- **Strengthening human rights institutions**

A wide range of USAID rule of law programming supports the protection of human rights as an integral component of promoting the rule of law, through reforming laws, strengthening justice sector institutions, and expanding access to justice for vulnerable groups. Programs may also be specifically targeted at supporting specialized institutions that uphold human rights. These programs strengthen the capacity of governmental and non-governmental organizations that play a critical role in advocating for greater human rights protection, monitoring abuses, increasing public awareness of human rights issues, following specific cases of human rights abuse to hold perpetrators accountable, and securing greater human rights performance by authorities. For example, programs have trained human rights defenders, supported human rights NGOs, and established or strengthened human rights ombudsman offices, human rights ministries, and governmental human rights commissions.

- **Working with non-state justice institutions to improve access to justice**

The community-based nature of many non-state justice institutions makes them more physically and often more financially accessible to local populations. Non-state justice systems may be more familiar to individuals, as they may be conducted in local languages according to familiar norms, and they may enable more expeditious resolution of disputes. At the same time, common weaknesses in these systems such as a lack of uniformity, capture by elite interests, and the presence of discriminatory practices may undercut fairness. Programs in this area can help build on the strengths of non-state systems to improve access to justice, while seeking to minimize the potential for unfairness and abuse. Examples include working with non-state systems to provide information about human rights and justice issues, supporting paralegals and NGOs to bridge state and non-state justice institutions, establishing linkages between state and non-state institutions, and improving oversight of non-state justice institutions.

- **Gender issues**

In the rule of law context, rights of women should be closely assessed. In many societies, due to cultural or religious influences, women do not enjoy the same rights as men. In addition, in every country some are victims of domestic violence, trafficking, or sex-related crimes. There are important UN treaties binding most countries which require equal treatment for men and women, and generally prohibit all discrimination, such as the Convention on the Elimination of All Forms of Discrimination Against Women (CEDAW). In those countries, rule of law assessments should not only look at the status of women from a legal perspective (extent of discrimination, problem of domestic violence, any domestic laws which violate CEDAW or other human rights instruments protecting the rights of women), but also their representation in the justice system (judges, prosecutors, lawyers, legal education faculties) and whether there are NGOs which actively advocate for women's rights. In addition, in recommending future rule of law programs, the assessment team should look for ways to promote gender issues (such as supporting gender equality-focused NGOs, justice monitoring, and advocacy related to domestic violence, family law issues, combating trafficking in persons, and inheritance rights, and advocating for greater women's representation in the justice system), or supporting the enactment of domestic legislation protecting the rights of women.

(5)   Effective Application

Justice sector programs can strengthen this element by supporting the following:

- **Improving investigative capacity of police and prosecutors**

Criminal laws are enforced by police and prosecutors, although in many civil law systems, investigating judges have the most important role in this regard. USAID has not funded many programs focused on improving the enforcement of criminal laws for the sake of enforcement alone (i.e. with the ultimate purpose of apprehending more criminals). Rather, these programs have focused on strengthening the ability of police and prosecutors to play their respective roles in new criminal justice systems.[23] In accusatorial criminal justice systems, the new role of the police is to provide evidence for a court process, which necessitates that they become much better investigators. Therefore, they need skills in interviewing, report writing, protecting and managing crime scenes, forensics, and respecting the chain of custody. The new role of the prosecutors is to present a compelling case against a defendant, which necessitates not just more knowledge of how to investigate a crime, but better knowledge of the criminal procedure code, oral advocacy skills, and other competencies. Often, there is a need to foster better cooperation between police and prosecutors in investigating crimes and prosecuting alleged perpetrators. Prosecutors can provide valuable training to police in the areas of rules of evidence and report writing, for example.

The Department of State's Bureau for International Narcotics and Law Enforcement (INL), often in partnership with the Department of Justice's Office of Overseas Prosecutorial Development Assistance and Training (OPDAT) and International Criminal Investigative Training Assistance Program (ICITAP), funds many programs that aim explicitly at improving the enforcement of criminal laws to suppress crime, especially transnational crime. INL's programs not only target the ability to investigate and prosecute crime, but they often target crime that may be considered complex, new to law enforcement in cooperating countries and central to transnational criminal operations, such as money laundering. Many of these programs providing assistance in improving witness protection, a key requirement for successful prosecution of complex or organized crime cases. Missions that want to address gaps in enforcement of the criminal laws in their country should consult *Assistance for Civilian Policing: USAID Policy Guidance* (December 2005) and investigate programs that INL is implementing or planning.

- **Enforcing judgments**

---

[23] The distinguishing characteristic of the new systems is that they are "accusatorial." They rely on two opposing viewpoints, in a process controlled by a neutral arbiter (the judge) and decided by a neutral party (the judge or jury).

If judicial decisions are not enforced, then the law has not been applied effectively. In the civil arena, enforcement of judgments is often carried out by enforcement personnel in the courts, overseen by a judge. In some cases, an executive agency is dedicated to enforcement. Many USAID missions have undertaken projects to improve the enforcement of judgments, in growing recognition that poor enforcement is a significant bottleneck to the rule of law. In the criminal sphere, much of the responsibility for enforcement of judgments falls to the correctional system. USAID is prohibited from working with prisons, other than through multilateral or regional organizations or through activities such as improving prison sanitation and ensuring the availability of adequate food, drinking water, and medical care for prisoners.[24]

- **Strengthening the implementation of administrative law and procedure**

While *reform* of administrative law speaks to fairness, *implementation* of the administrative law process speaks to effective application. Virtually every citizen interfaces with government functions and is affected by the administrative law system. Therefore, as *Using Administrative Law Tools and Concepts to Strengthen USAID Programming* (2008) points out, effective implementation can "make democracy relevant" or "help democracy deliver." Implementation of administrative law can particularly benefit the poor and vulnerable groups, since it is these groups who may face the greatest obstacles to using the administrative law system in addressing their everyday needs. Examples of programming include implementing access to information and open meetings laws in Georgia, providing training and technical assistance to agency appeal authorities and administrative judges in Bosnia and Herzegovina and helping the Ombudsman's Office in Peru to deal with complaints against administrative decision-makers on housing, utilities, and other matters.

Table 1 below summarizes illustrative program support options. A key factor in determining which option to choose will be costs or resource constraints. Depending on the available budget for justice reform in a particular country, some useful program support options will unfortunately not be possible. In making recommendations, the assessment team should conduct cost-benefit analyses and focus on program support which is the most likely to positively impact the justice system.

---

[24] See *supra* note 13.

Table 1: Summary of Illustrative Program Support Options

Element of Rule of Law	Program Support Options
Order and Security	• Establishing, rebuilding or expanding justice institutions • Crime prevention, community security and civilian policing • Disarmament, demobilization and reintegration • Witness and court personnel protection programs
Legitimacy	• Constitutional drafting processes • Legal reform commissions and other forms of citizen mobilization • Harmonization of customary or religious law with the state body of law • Transitional justice mechanisms to address past abuses
Checks and Balances	• Establishing or strengthening independent judicial bodies • Upgrading or reforming judicial career processes • Improving working conditions for judicial personnel • Strengthening judicial administration, management and self-governance • Strengthening independent judicial and legal professional associations • Enhancing judicial professional development and access to the laws • Stimulating citizen support for judicial independence • Legislative strengthening
Fairness	• Reforming and implementing procedural codes • Reforming administrative law • Improving transparent and efficient administration of justice system components • Expanding access to legal services • Improving the quality of private defense • Improving the accessibility of the state justice system • Supporting or expanding alternative dispute resolution • Increasing citizen awareness of human rights standards and issues • Strengthening human rights institutions
Effective Application	• Improving investigative capacity of and cooperation between police and prosecutors • Enforcing judgments • Strengthening the implementation of administrative law and procedure

APPENDIX A: ILLUSTRATIVE ASSESSMENT QUESTIONS

Essential Elements of Rule of Law	Framework of Laws	Justice Sector Institutions
Order and Security	**What is the legal basis for maintaining order? Are the constitution or other basic laws in effect? Is society under martial law or other exceptional law (e.g., laws of foreign occupation, UN Security Council Resolution)? Is a cease-fire or peace accord working?** **If constitutional order is effective, how effective are the criminal code and criminal procedure code?** **Do police/prosecutors have sufficient legal authority to investigate and prosecute crime, including complex cases such as organized crime, drug and human trafficking and financial crimes? Is there a modern criminal code which conforms to international standards and provides a sufficient basis for dealing with most types of crime?** **Do the prescribed procedures for trying criminal cases (usually in a criminal procedure code) provide the basis for conducting trials within a reasonable period of time? Are prescribed procedures appropriate to the seriousness of the offense? Are minor offenses tried under simpler, speedier procedures than are used for more serious offenses?**	**Are citizens and foreigners safe? Are crime rates rising, remaining the same or declining? Do police control crime or contribute to crime? Do citizens trust and actively assist police in solving crime? Do citizens engage in vigilantism of any kind?** **Is there an effective police force? Do police cooperate well with prosecutors and the courts in the gathering of evidence and prosecution of criminal cases?** **Do prosecutors try cases effectively in practice? Do prosecutors have the knowledge and skills required to present criminal cases effectively and properly? Are charges brought only when there is adequate evidence of the commission of a crime? Are a large number of cases dismissed for lack of adequate evidence or because of unfounded or incorrect charges?** **What are the three major crime/security threats in the country?** **How can the coordination between police investigators and prosecutors be improved?** **Describe a case that was successfully prosecuted due to good coordination between police and prosecutors.** **Describe a case that failed because of poor coordination between police and prosecutors.** **What are some of the biggest weaknesses that judges find with criminal cases that come before**

		their courts?
		Are there forensic means to analyze physical evidence? If so, describe.
		Can circumstantial evidence be used to prosecute cases? If so, describe.
		Is plea bargaining possible under current law?
		Is a tracking system (either paper or automated)in place that monitors how long prisoners are kept in remand before being charged with a crime, and how long those that are charged with a crime wait in prison before going to trial? If so, describe.
		Are people being held on remand imprisoned with convicts?
		Are there any programs that explain to citizens how the criminal justice system should work and what their rights are within the system?
		Is joint training ever conducted that includes police, prosecutors, and magistrates/judges?
		What are the policies on use of informants?
		Are there racketeering laws for investigating organized crime?
		Does the police agency have a use of force policy in effect?
		Is the concept of the force continuum taught to police?
		Are there current policies and procedures in place for the police?
		Are the police capable of conducting interviews and interrogations while respecting human rights and human dignity?

		How do the police identify and train instructors?
		Do police instructors train their replacements before being reassigned?
		Do police receive training in crime scene protection?
Legitimacy	What is the source of law? What is its history? What groups in society wrote the laws?	How long have the key institutions been in place? How are they viewed by the public? How are they viewed by different social groups?
	How are the laws viewed today by different social groups? Are any laws resisted?	Which institutions command respect, disrespect or fear? How do they rate against other institutions in the state or society? Is law respected by elites? Do elites suffer if they break the law?
	How long has the constitution been in effect? How often has it been amended? Have amendments been made by a process which includes a genuine opportunity for public participation and decision-making?	Do the courts and other elements of the justice system enforce law in a way that favors certain persons or groups over others? Do judges consistently favor certain persons or groups in society over others when making decisions on civil matters (such as in debt collection, landlord-tenant, or land and property rights cases) or in determining guilt or innocence and punishments in criminal cases?
	Do substantial portions of the population conduct activities outside of the formal legal system? For example, is there a substantial amount of economic activity going on which is unregulated by the legal system (e.g., a large informal sector, gray or black market, or unregulated lending)? Is this due to laws that create unreasonable barriers to legal entry into the market for substantial segments of the population or businesses?	Do the actions of the courts reflect a heavy bias in favor of the government's position in almost all cases that come before them (whether civil, criminal, or administrative)? Do members of certain social or economic classes nearly always receive preferential treatment in the legal system over others? Does a substantial portion of the population believe that the formal legal institutions serve the interests of only a few privileged persons or groups?
	Do portions of the population resort to self- help (such as shootings, lynching, or other violence) to protect their property or personal rights or to punish transgressors? Do they carry out these actions because adequate legal remedies are not provided in the law itself in such cases or because the law provides for	What role do customary, religious, or community institutions play in practice in the justice sector? Are they regarded as more legitimate

| | immunity for certain persons or groups?

What is the place of customary or religious law? Is it recognized as part of the country's laws, or is its status unclear? Is it written, codified, or otherwise documented? Does it conflict with laws which are part of the formally adopted legal system, or generally accepted international human rights standards? If it does conflict with the official framework of laws, do substantial portions of the population nevertheless regard it as having priority over the official legal codes? | and credible than institutions of the state? Do judges, prosecutors, and lawyers understand and properly apply customary and religious law (where it has been officially adopted as part of the country's legal framework)?

Do customary or traditional institutions play a role in mediating disputes outside the formal justice system or in restorative justice?

Do prosecutors use their authority to bring charges fairly and impartially based on credible evidence? Do they prosecute or not prosecute individuals or organizations for political, social, corrupt, or other illegitimate reasons (or are they perceived as acting in this way)? Do they consistently fail to act to protect certain persons or groups from rights violations?

Do police and other bodies performing law enforcement and public order functions consistently act within the law? Do police routinely violate human rights with relative impunity? Do courts routinely accept and consider illegally obtained evidence (coerced confessions or items obtained as the result of illegal searches)? Are armed forces held legally accountable for their actions when performing law enforcement or public safety functions? Are there armed groups that harm and intimidate citizens with seeming impunity? |
| Checks and Balances | Do the constitution and laws of the country provide that the judiciary is an independent branch of government? Do the laws relating to the structure and operations of the judiciary place the principal control over most judicial operations in the hands of the judiciary itself?

Does the law provide for a | Is the independence of the judiciary respected in practice?

How problematic is executive interference with the independence of the judiciary?

Do high ranking government officials frequently and strongly criticize the courts, judges or their decisions? Are sudden audits and |

selection system for judges and prosecutors that limits the ability of the executive and the legislature to make appointments based primarily on political considerations? Are judges entitled to security of tenure? In other words, are they entitled to serve until such time as certain specifically defined events occur (e.g., attaining a fixed retirement age, disability or removal for cause)? Do the laws permit unlimited executive discretion in the provision of pay, benefits and allowances to judges, prosecutors and other public officials in the legal system? Or are compensation and benefits clearly fixed by law?

Once appointed, can judges be removed for non-feasance or malfeasance in the performance of their duties? By law, do judges enjoy sufficient immunity to carry out their duties free of interference or harassment? Are the grounds for discipline and removal of judges and prosecutors clearly defined in laws? Are disciplinary and removal decisions transparent and made by a body and process that is not under the exclusive control of the executive and legislature? Are disciplinary and removal decisions subject to judicial review?

Is there a law on freedom of information? Does it apply to all branches of the government (for example, the U.S. Freedom of Information Act [FOIA] applies only to the executive branch of the U.S. Government)?

Do existing laws provide for appropriate external and internal oversight mechanisms for reviewing and acting upon

inspections of court operations (usually by the Ministry of Justice) used to intimidate judges? Are changes in pay, allowances and court budgets used to reward judges supporting the government's position or to punish judges making decisions that are politically unpopular or contrary to the interests of the government?

To what extent do judges or prosecutors leave their positions before the end of their terms? Why?

Do influential officials engage in "telephone justice?" Under what circumstances?

Are police accountable to civilians? At what levels? Are there internal or external (civilian) boards that review police conduct? Do these bodies aggressively review and act upon complaints of misconduct?

Does civil society oversee or monitor the justice system, or advocate for change? Does the media cover it? What is the role of the bar?

Are judges and prosecutors harassed, intimidated or attacked? By whom? Is witness intimidation or cooperation a problem? Does the government make reasonable efforts to provide personal protection to judges, prosecutors, lawyers and witnesses? Are courthouses secure? Are threats or acts of violence against judges, prosecutors and witnesses aggressively investigated and punished?

Does the body that disciplines and removes judges and prosecutors act fairly, openly and impartially? Are its decisions based solely on the criteria established by law for discipline and removal? Does it aggressively investigate complaints

	complaints of police brutality or other misconduct? Are there legally recognized and binding codes of conduct in effect for judges, prosecutors and lawyers?	of misconduct, malfeasance and non-feasance and resolve them in a timely manner? Are a significant number of judges, prosecutors and lawyers disciplined or removed each year? If there are ethics and conduct codes in effect for judges, prosecutors and lawyers, are there mechanisms that ensure that such codes are effectively enforced?
Fairness		
Equal application	Does the law, as written, discriminate against or favor different groups? Why? Is such discrimination reasonable and consistent with international standards? How could it be? Are women better protected under the laws of the formal legal system than under customary law? Are their rights adequately protected under either of them?	Are all parties treated the same in the courtroom? Do judges and other parties act with decorum and with respect for all parties? Are judges' rulings consistent regardless of the status of the parties before the court? Do members of certain nationality, ethnic, religious, social, or economically disadvantaged groups make up a disproportionately high number of all persons in pre-trial confinement? Are vulnerable victims, such as in trafficking in persons cases, treated with dignity and compassion by police, prosecutors and judges?
Protection of rights	Which human rights treaties has the state ratified? Does the framework of laws in the country recognize these rights and provide for means of enforcing them? If the country is not a signatory to international human rights treaties, does its constitution nevertheless recognize basic human rights generally recognized by international law? Have subordinate laws been passed providing for institutions and procedures to enforce those rights? Does the criminal law provide	Do domestic and international monitoring organizations report significant violations of human rights by government institutions, including the police and security services? Are human and other rights established by law well understood and consistently respected and protected in practice by the courts, prosecutors and police? Do members of the public understand their basic human rights as guaranteed by their constitution and international law? What are the mechanisms for

	for periodic review of the decision to keep an individual in pre-trial detention by someone other than the prosecutor or police and in accordance with internationally accepted standards? To obtain release from pre-trial detention, do criminal procedures place the burden of proof on the state or on the accused? Does the criminal law provide for reasonable alternatives to detention pending trial?	protecting human rights? Is there a human rights ombudsman or agency, and is this institution effective? Is there a constitutional court that effectively protects human rights? Does the government (including other courts) respect and enforce its judgments? Do domestic and international non-governmental and media organizations effectively monitor the human rights situation and bring deficiencies to the attention of government officials and the public? Does the government respond to these reports, or does it routinely ignore or reject them? Does the government retaliate against individuals or groups raising human rights concerns?

What percentage of the population is in prison awaiting sentencing? Do individuals spend long periods of time in detention awaiting trial? Does this conform to international standards? Do courts and prosecutors appear, in practice, to be biased in favor of holding persons in detention while awaiting trial? Are alternatives to pre-trial detention (where allowed by law) seriously considered and accepted for some accused? Are detention decisions made by courts reviewed at higher levels and overturned when inappropriate? |
| *Procedural fairness* | Are the laws prescribing the procedures to be followed in civil and criminal proceedings consistent with international fair trial standards?

Does the country's civil procedure code provide that parties to civil proceedings (such as disputes over land or personal property ownership, indebtedness, contract rights, compensation for personal injuries and family law matters) have the following rights: 1) to receive proper and timely | Are civil and criminal procedures, as set forth in the codes, consistently followed in practice? Do judges consistently respect the procedural rights of all parties and sanction those participants (lawyers, prosecutors, witnesses, and parties) who violate the rules? Are judges' decisions well-reasoned, supported by the evidence presented and consistent with all applicable law? In cases in which judges have discretion in the enforcement of trial procedures, do they exercise that discretion reasonably and in a way that |

	notice of all court proceedings; 2) to have a fair opportunity to present evidence and arguments in support of their case, review evidence and cross-examine witnesses; 3) to have their case decided within a reasonable period of time; and to appeal adverse judgments? Do existing laws provide sufficient authority to judges to ensure that these procedures are followed? Are prescribed procedures overly complex and unnecessarily time-consuming, especially with regard to the trial of cases in which the issues are simple or involve disputes of low monetary value? Does the criminal procedure code provide for a right to a speedy and public trial before an impartial judge, notice of all charges, right to review the prosecution's evidence and cross examine witnesses, right to present evidence and witnesses in defense, right to legal representation, a presumption of innocence, and a right against self-incrimination?	encourages the fair and expeditious resolution of cases? Is there a culture encouraging attorney proactiveness and effectiveness in protecting the procedural rights of clients in both civil and criminal cases?
Access	Do the constitution and laws include provisions providing that trials shall be open to the public (including the media)? Are any exceptions to that requirement carefully defined and limited? Are court fees established by law and published regulations? Are such fees reasonable, or do they limit access to court by lower income individuals or groups? Are there legally prescribed means for indigents and low-income parties to get waivers of filing and court fees? Does the constitution guarantee the right to legal counsel in legal proceedings,	Do most segments of society understand their legal rights and the role of the legal system in protecting them? Do they understand how the courts work and how to access them effectively? Do the courts have a sufficient number of courtrooms, or are most sessions held in the offices of judges or other places? What mechanisms are in place for defense of indigents accused of crimes (such as public defenders service or court-appointed counsel)? Does the mechanism used provide, in practice, competent legal counsel for indigents who are criminally

	and legal counsel for indigents at government expense in criminal proceedings? Have laws been passed that provide mechanisms for providing such counsel? Is there any right to legal counsel or legal assistance in civil cases for indigent persons?	accused? Do women use the justice system, and what are the results? Are they discouraged from reporting domestic violence or sex-related crimes? What types of discrimination or obstacles do they face? Where do poor people and other social groups and classes go to obtain justice? Is free or affordable legal advice available to medium- or low-income groups on civil matters (such as family, contract or property law)? Are most citizens represented by legal counsel when they go into court, or do many represent themselves in court (*pro se* representation)? Do the courts provide assistance of any kind to such parties? Does the local bar association provide any kind of low- or no-cost (*pro bono*) legal services to individuals or groups? Are the courts user-friendly and customer service-oriented? Are court intake offices conveniently located and efficiently organized? Is there sufficient court staff to provide information to the public? Are there publicly available directories of court personnel? Are hearing schedules regularly posted? Are court filing fees publicly posted? Are standards of conduct for court staff personnel displayed in intake areas? Have measures been taken to assure the physical safety of parties, witnesses, and the public while in the courthouse? Do lawyers have the knowledge and skills necessary to advise parties competently and advocate their interests in court? What judicial or administrative recourse do citizens or small business have against state

		actions? What recourse do they have against abuses by the judiciary, prosecution or police?
Effective Application	Do civil procedure codes and other laws relating to the enforcement of civil judgments prescribe clear responsibilities and well-defined and efficient procedures for enforcement of civil judgments? Is sufficient legal authority provided to judges and enforcement agents (e.g., marshals, bailiffs, sheriffs, debt collection agents, and police) to enforce judgments effectively? Do enforcement laws include provisions permitting a judge to issue interim orders freezing or otherwise protecting assets pending final judgment? Does the law permit parties to reopen and re-litigate the case as part of enforcement proceedings? Do civil procedure laws permit parties to make unlimited appeals to the highest court of all rulings made by the enforcement judge or agent during the enforcement proceedings (rather than holding all appeals until final decisions are made)? Are there significant delays in the process as a result? Can courts issue injunctions against actions of the executive and legislative branches? Can they issue injunctions against actions by private interests?	Are civil cases tried effectively and in a timely manner? Are there significant delays in the trials of cases and substantial case backlogs? Are case disposition times in line with recognized standards for courts in the region? Are judges proactive in reducing trial delays (such as limiting continuances, sanctioning non-appearing parties and ensuring proper service of process)? Are judges fully knowledgeable about the applicable laws and trial procedures? Are decisions consistently well-reasoned and legally correct? Are a substantial number of cases reversed on appeal and returned for retrial? Is case document processing by court staffs inefficient and excessively time-consuming? Does the judiciary collect timely, usable data on the performance of the courts? Does it collect information that shows the workload of judges, the time to disposition, the type of disposition, the type of case, the parties? Are these data used in drawing up the budget? If not, what information is used to prepare the budget? Is there a sufficient number of judges, prosecutors and court personnel? Is redistribution of existing personnel warranted in light of current workloads (e.g. busy urban courts v. slow rural ones)? In practice, are civil judgments enforced in an effective and timely manner? If not, why not? Are judges and other parties knowledgeable about civil procedure rules, and do they apply them properly in practice? Do the courts permit parties to introduce new evidence and arguments and

		effectively re-litigate the original case during the enforcement process? Are enforcement agencies provided sufficient personnel, training, facilities, budget and other resources necessary to carry out their responsibilities effectively?
		Do enforcement agencies (other than courts—bailiffs, sheriffs, and marshals) aggressively and effectively satisfy judgments within a reasonable time? Does corruption affect the enforcement process? If prosecutors or police have any responsibility for enforcing civil judgments, do they cooperate with and adequately support the enforcement process?
		Can citizens bring suit and obtain relief against the state? Can they do so against powerful interests?

APPENDIX B: RULE OF LAW ASSESSMENT
SAMPLE SCOPE OF WORK

Purpose of Assessment

The purpose of this solicitation is to assist USAID to conduct a targeted analysis of the status of rule of law development in Country X, and an assessment of the primary opportunities and constraints to the further development of the rule of law in Country X. The assessment will lead directly into a strategy for rule of law assistance in Country X that includes the priority areas that could benefit from USAID intervention, and prioritized recommendations for programming.

Background and Context

Statement of Work

The purpose of this assessment is to provide USAID with an analysis of the primary challenges in advancing the rule of law in order to develop a strategy for programming. It includes two main tasks:

1) An analysis of the primary challenges and opportunities in advancing the rule of law, including an assessment of political will for reform
2) A proposed strategy for programming, including prioritized areas of intervention and program recommendations

The contractor shall conduct a background review of key documents, as well as on-site research and interviews to develop a report that addresses these areas. The assessment will be consistent with the *Rule of Law Strategic Framework*, which is designed to synchronize with the mission's broader DG strategy.

The report will include the following components:

1) Analysis of primary challenges and opportunities in advancing the rule of law:
This section of the report will analyze the current state of the justice sector as a basis for deriving strategic recommendations. Consistent with the draft *Rule of Law Strategic Framework*, the analysis will include the following four steps:

First, the assessment will take into account the political and historic context, including current events. It will briefly outline the political, governance and legal structure of the country as it relates to the current state of the legal framework and justice sector institutions, and identify recent changes that help frame the rule of law problems to be addressed. This section is intended to succinctly situate the rule of law in the broader political economy of the country.

The second step will be to evaluate the roles and interests of the major political actors, and assess the political will for judicial reform. The purpose of this part of the analysis will be to identify who is likely to "win" and "lose" from the enactment of reforms to the rule of law system. Identifying the winners and losers in light of their potential power will be instructive in terms of assessing the level of political will for various types of interventions.

Step three will examine program options beyond the justice sector that might have a bearing on the rule of law. Such considerations will include issues such as lack of consensus over governance, lack of competition in political processes, inadequate inclusion of members of society, and inability to govern effectively. The purpose of this section will be to identify other corollary impediments to democratic transition outside the justice sector that condition potential progress in the justice sector.

Step four will assess the justice sector itself. This will include examination of the five key elements that comprise the rule of law, namely: 1) order and security, 2) legitimacy, 3) checks and balances, 4) fairness, 5) effective application. Each of these five elements must be present for rule of law to prevail. This section will focus on how these elements are embodied and enacted within the legal framework and justice sector institutions and actors. This section should outline the key features of the justice system, including the framework of laws and the justice sector institutions. The analysis should also address key challenges and opportunities for promoting the essential elements of the rule of law within the legal framework and justice sector institutions. The purpose of this section will be to identify potential points of intervention within the justice system itself that are in need of reform and amenable to change.

In addition, the assessment will review existing USG and other donor programs in the justice sector, to determine what progress has been made so far, and where opportunities and entry points might exist for programming.

2) Programming Strategy
The assessment will inform the development of a strategy and programmatic options for rule of law interventions. This will be based on the findings from the preceding sections as well as additional considerations such as USAID local mission priorities, USG policy, availability of resources, and activities of other donors. It will be designed to focus rule of law activities around the primary challenges in promoting the rule of law in light of the current state of political will, opportunities and constraints for reform, and past successes.

The strategy should include the following components:
- Primary rule of law problem(s) framed in terms of the essential element(s) of the rule of law that are most critical to establishing the rule of law in Country X.
- Opportunities for intervention, including the specific institutions and laws for which opportunities exist for reform.
- Program recommendations including intended results that should be achieved through follow-on programs to address the primary rule of law problem. Recommendations should be prioritized in order of importance.

Methodology

The contractor shall provide a three-person team to work directly with USAID staff to conduct the work in three stages.

Preparation phase: The first phase of the assessment will involve reviewing background materials and key documents; developing an assessment and evaluation methodology that includes primary research questions and interview protocols; and preparing a schedule of interviews for the subsequent field work stage. A pre-trip meeting with relevant USAID staff is required during the preparation phase to review documents, discuss background reviews and come to agreement on the primary research questions, interview protocols and assessment schedule. This meeting will take place preferably at the USAID offices in Washington, DC, but may be conducted via teleconference if necessary. At least three working days per team-member are authorized for the preparation phase.

Field-work phase: The team will conduct at least 18 days of field research, including gathering and reviewing documents and data, and conducting structured interviews with key informants (and focus groups, if appropriate) and beneficiaries, including the Judiciary, Government personnel, international and donor personnel, USAID partners, members of Parliament, lawyers, judges, court administrators, mediators, civil society organizations, citizens groups, the media, and other relevant stakeholders. The team will present a list of interviewees to USAID for approval prior to conducting interviews. The contractor will be responsible for developing the list of interviewees and arranging meetings, as well as transportation to the meetings. USAID will provide one or two staff members to participate in the field-work phase of the assessment.

Report-writing Phase: The contractor will draft the assessment report, which will include all of the components outlined above. The draft report shall be submitted for formal USAID review within ten working days after departure of the contractor from the country. USAID will have ten working days to provide comments to the contractor. The final report shall be submitted no more than ten working days thereafter. A total of at least eight working days per team member are authorized for the report-writing phase.

Deliverables

The contractor shall provide the following deliverables to USAID.

1. Literature Review and Evaluation/Assessment Methodology
Prior to beginning the interview process, the contractor shall prepare for the assessment by reviewing key documents on the justice sector; background material on the political situation; and applicable sections of USAID and project documentation. The contractor will also prepare a methodology plan including primary research questions, interview protocols to structure the interviews, and a list of proposed individuals to be interviewed. The methodology plan, interview schedules, and interview protocol will be presented to USAID staff prior to departure for the field-research phase.

2. Oral Briefings (two)
The contractor will provide two briefings for USAID staff, including an introductory briefing within two days of arrival in country, and an exit briefing presenting the team's findings and recommendations to USAID prior to departure.

3. Draft Report.   The assessment team will present a draft report in English of its findings and recommendations to USAID within ten working days from the time of departure. The draft report will be no more than 40 pages. The report will include all of the components outlined above, although not necessarily in the order specified above.

4. Final Report.   The Final Report will be provided to USAID in electronic format in MS Word and Adobe PDF, within 10 calendar days following receipt of comments from USAID. An electronic copy and 5 hard copies shall be provided to USAID. The report shall include all of the components outlined above, although not necessarily in the order specified above. The report shall also include an executive summary and not exceed 40 pages (excluding appendices). Appendices should at a minimum include the scope of work for the evaluation; a list of individuals interviewed; a complete description of the methodology used for the evaluation; and any questionnaires used.

The report shall follow USAID branding procedures.

The contractor shall also submit a copy of the final report to PPC/CDIE/DI.

Team Composition and Qualifications

The assessment will be carried out by a three person team. The team shall include:

- A team leader (Expatriate) with a professional background in international development work, including rule of law development. This person shall be responsible for coordinating and directing the overall assessment effort, including preparation and submission of the draft and final assessment reports. He/she should have a minimum of 10 years experience in the design, implementation, and/or evaluation of foreign assistance programs including USAID-related rule of law programs. As assessment team leader, the incumbent should be thoroughly familiar with techniques of program impact appraisals and possess good organization and team-building skills. The team leader should have excellent written and oral communication skills in English. Previous overseas experience in the region and knowledge of the language is desirable.

- A team member (Expatriate) with at least 5 years of relevant experience in rule of law development and/or democracy and governance assistance, possessing strong background knowledge of the region and experience in the design, implementation and/or evaluation of foreign assistance programs. Strong writing and word processing skills are a requirement. Previous overseas experience in the region and knowledge of the language is desirable.

- A Team Member (local): A lawyer, political scientist, public sector management specialist, or researcher. Minimum degree BA in Law or related field. Good understanding of political dynamics, the legal framework, justice institutions, Rule of Law actors and political actors in the country is essential. At least three years' work experience required. Knowledge of USAID and other donors is preferable.

At least one of the two expatriate team members must have previous overseas experience in the region and some knowledge of the language.

USAID will appoint one USAID/DCHA/DG staff member and one USAID/mission staff member to participate in the assessment, including in all meetings during the field research stage.

The contractor will certify that there is no conflict of interest or potential conflict of interest with respect to the performance of this assessment on the part of the contractor and the contractor's team members. The contractor will guarantee that substitutions will not be made for individuals proposed as team members without the approval of USAID.

Period of Performance

The work called for in this scope will start on X and will be completed approximately 10 weeks later. The field work will start on X.

The mission will respond to the content of the assessment with oral comments at the debriefing and will provide written comments within 3 weeks of receipt of the draft report.

Logistical support

All logistical support will be provided by the contractor including travel, transportation, secretarial and office support, interpretation, report printing and communication, as appropriate.

Workweek

A 6-day work week is authorized in the field with no premium pay.

Technical Direction

Technical direction during the performance of this delivery order will be provided by X.

REFERENCES

Carothers, Thomas (ed.), *Promoting the Rule of Law Abroad: In Search of Knowledge*, Carnegie Endowment for International Peace, 2006.

Hammergren, Linn, *Assessments, Monitoring, Evaluation, and Research: Improving the Knowledge Base for Judicial Reform Programs*, USAID, 1998.

Hammergren, Linn *Political Will, Constituency Building, and Public Support in Rule of Law Programs*, USAID, August 1998.

Hammergren, Linn, *Do Judicial Councils Further Judicial Reform? Lessons from Latin America*, Carnegie Endowment for International Peace, June 2002.

Glendon, Mary Ann et al., *Comparative Legal Traditions*, West Group, 1999.

Golub , Steven, *Beyond Rule of Law Orthodoxy: The Legal Empowerment Alternative*, Carnegie Endowment for International Peace, Rule of Law Series Number 41, October 2003.

Prilliman, William C., *The Judiciary and Democratic Decay in Latin America: Declining Confidence in the Rule of Law*, Praeger Publishers, 2000.

Reiling, Dory, Linn Hammergren and Adrian Di Giovanni, *Justice Sector Assessments: A Handbook*, The World Bank, 2008.

Stromseth, Jane, David Wippman and Rosa Brooks, *Can Might Make Rights?: Building the Rule of Law after Military Interventions*, Cambridge University Press, 2006.

Transparency International, *Combating Corruption in Judicial Systems: Advocacy Toolkit*, 2008.

Trebilcock, Michael J., and Ronald J. Daniels, *Rule of Law Reform and Development: Charting the Fragile Path of Progress*, Edward Elgar Publishing, Inc., Northampton, MA, 2008.

United Nations Security Council, *The Rule of Law and Transitional Justice in Conflict and Post Conflict Societies: Report of the Secretary General*, August 3, 2004

Upham, Frank, *Mythmaking in the Rule of Law Orthodoxy*, Carnegie Endowment for International Peace, Rule of Law Series Number 30, September 2002.

USAID, *Achievements in Building and Maintaining the Rule of Law: MSI's Studies in LAC, E&E, AFR, and ANE*, November 2002.

USAID, *Alternative Dispute Resolution Practitioners' Guide*, March 1998.

USAID, *Case Tracking and Management Guide*, September 2001.

USAID, *Conducting a DG Assessment: A Framework for Strategy Development*, November 2000.

USAID, *Foreign Aid in the National Interest: Promoting Freedom, Security, and Opportunity*, 2002.

USAID, *Enforcement of Judgments: A Toolkit for Assessment and Programming*, forthcoming.

USAID, *Guidance for Promoting Judicial Independence and Impartiality*, January 2002.

USAID, *Guide to Court Reform and the Role of Court Personnel*, forthcoming.

USAID, *Improving Access to Justice through Non-State Justice Institutions: Issues to Consider*, forthcoming.

USAID, *Legal Empowerment of the Poor: From Concepts to Assessment*, March 2007.

USAID, *Promoting Security Sector Reform in Fragile States*, April 2005.

USAID, *Policy Guidance on Assistance for Civilian Policing*, December 2005.

USAID, *Rebuilding the Rule of Law in Post-conflict Environments*, forthcoming.

USAID, *USAID Anti-Corruption Strategy*, January 2005.

USAID, *Using Administrative Law Tools and Concepts to Strengthen USAID Programming: A Guide for USAID Democracy and Governance Officers*, 2008.

USAID, *Weighing in on the Scales of Justice: Strategic Approaches for Donor-Supported Rule of Law Programs*, 1994.

Vera Institute of Justice, *Measuring Progress Toward Safety and Justice: A Global Guide to the Design of Performance Indicators across the Justice Sector*, Vera Institute of Justice, November, 2003.

The U.S. Agency for International Development (USAID) is an independent federal agency that receives overall foreign policy guidance from the Secretary of State. For more than 40 years, USAID has been the principal U.S. agency to extend assistance to countries recovering from disaster, trying to escape poverty, and engaging in democratic reforms.

USAID supports long-term and equitable economic growth and advances U.S. foreign policy objectives by supporting:
- Economic growth, agriculture, and trade
- Global health
- Democracy and conflict prevention
- Humanitarian assistance

The Agency's strength is its field offices located in five regions of the world:
- Sub-Saharan Africa
- Asia
- Middle East
- Latin America and the Caribbean
- Europe and Eurasia